300 Innovative SOCCER Drills
for
Total PLAYER Development

by
Roger Wilkinson and Mick Critchell

Library of Congress Cataloging Number

by Critchell, Mick and Wilkinson, Roger
     300 Innovative SOCCER Drills for Total PLAYER Development

ISBN No. 1-890946-36-2
Library of Congress Catalog Number 00-101984
Copyright © June 2000

Art Direction/Layout	Kimberly N. Bender
Editing and Proofing	Bryan R. Beaver
Printed by	DATA REPRODUCTIONS Auburn Hills, Michigan

REEDSWAIN INC
612 Pughtown Road
Spring City, Pennsylvania 19475
1-800-331-5191
www.reedswain.com

300 Innovative SOCCER Drills
for
Total PLAYER Development

by
Roger Wilkinson

*Luton Town, European "A" license coach,
FIFA Coach
New Zealand National Under 20 Coach
Technical Director New Zealand football.*

and
Mick Critchell

*Certificate of Physical Education, Carnegie
College, Leeds
Former Head of Physical Education, Harriet
Costello School, Basingstoke
Coach to Farnborough Town Football Club
Fitness Adviser*

published by REEDSWAIN INC

TABLE OF CONTENTS

INTRODUCTION

"If we do what we did yesterday we will be beaten; if we do what others are doing today we can be competitive, but if we fill each day with initiative, we will be the best." This is a quote from Robert De Castella, the ex-Director of the Australian Institute of Sport at his farewell press conference and, for me, sums up the malaise in British sport, particularly soccer, because most coaches are still doing what they did yesterday.

Soccer training in this country is often old fashioned and outdated. The sports scientist and exercise specialist are rarely allowed access to players, and managers and coaches continue to rely on methods and practices they were brought up on as players. There is a lack of careful planning and very little innovation from those running the game. It is interesting to see that the most enlightened managers appear to be those who have played abroad.

Soccer is not a science and I would not want it to be, but there is no doubt that science can help improve the level of soccer. Training is very demanding, so it is important that time is not wasted on sessions which have little relevance to soccer. To make sure the training session is successful, it is vital that the coach has proper and realistic aims before he starts. If he does not, then instead of a serious but enjoyable and demanding workout, it can become a worthless time-filler resulting in little or no improvement in performance.

In recent years the importance of fitness and work-rate has been criticized by some people in the game. They argue that if we concentrated on skills, then everything would fall into place. I believe that this is an incorrect assumption. To be successful a player has to have a high level of technical skill, physical fitness and tactical skill. A player who is weak in one area might compensate by being strong in another. This may not matter for the schoolboy or amateur player. However, the higher up the ladder a player moves, particularly in semi-pro and professional soccer, the less he can get away with a weakness in technique, tactics or fitness, because all 3 are related. When a player gets tired and fatigue of the central nervous system becomes a problem, technique and co-ordination fall away. Similarly, if technique is poor, then more energy is wasted and endurance is lost much more quickly. Successful use of tactics also relies on good technique and physical fitness. How often do we see a clever tactical maneuver break down due to an inaccurate pass, lack of speed or poor anticipation by an individual?

Soccer is developing all the time and players have to be better athletes than they were a few years ago. Other countries have gone forward in this area, through improved and more scientific training methods and they now match the pace, physical strength and "never say die" attitude of our players. It was interesting to read the comments of Walter Smith, the Rangers manager, after Juventus had beaten Rangers twice in the European Cup during the 1995-96 season. "You were looking at players who are far, far stronger in terms of muscle development than anything we've got. One of the key lessons for me in these matches with Juventus is that we are lagging behind physically now and that puts us in really deep trouble. The gulf in technical capacity is widened because they have made themselves superior athletes. I feel a change in our approach is essential. We must scrap all our assumptions about having a physical edge and realize we have, in fact, a serious deficit to make up. Obviously we must go on striving for improved technique, but that will be harder to attain than the physical improvements and, in any case, it won't help us sufficiently if we don't get fitter and stronger at the same time. I'm talking about a scientific approach to giving our players the athletic capacity to apply whatever skills they have to the maximum."

If we are to improve the fitness, strength and power of players in this country, we must employ coaches and fitness experts who have a basic knowledge, understand the different components of fitness, but, above all, are able to analyze soccer movements and so integrate a function of fitness training into the overall training program. Some progress has been made in this direction with the employment of track coaches, who have ensured that players warm up properly and have incorporated essential strength training programs into the fitness sessions. However, they are athletic coaches and you cannot train soccer players the same as track athletes! On average, players change direction every 5 seconds and the mean sprint in a game is seventeen yards. Therefore, having players run one hundred yards in a straight line has little relevance to what actually happens in a game.

Professional clubs should also be employing nutritionists, who advise on diet and fluid intake. I appreciate it is very difficult to change attitudes, particularly of those who have spent many years in the professional game, but it is a case of continually drip-feeding information and hoping that some of it sticks. Perhaps we have to start with the younger players and educate them, since they seem more receptive to new ideas. The half-time cup of tea and after-match beers, which are the norm for nearly every British soccer player, are part of a culture which needs drastic changing. We must produce players in this country who take pride in being professional athletes and accept the responsibilities that this brings. As Ossie Ardiles once remarked, "Like the Italians, you never saw Klinsman with a beer."

There is no doubt that the standard of soccer has improved throughout the world and there are few easy games at International level any more. This increase in standard has meant that even higher performance levels are required. With this increase in demand, training has to be continually improved and better organized so that players remain motivated and performances improve. It is not good enough for managers and coaches to decide what they are going to do as they turn up for the session. Too often they bow to the wishes of the players and allow them to dictate the pattern of the training. The result is

"If we do what we did yesterday we will be beaten; if we do what others are doing today we can be competitive, but if we fill each day with initiative, we will be the best."

usually small-sided games, with two small goals, or endless games of 'keep away'. The problem with this type of practice is that the outcome tends to be a concentration on short and elaborate passing, lots of back passes, a slow pace and hardly any wing play. Undoubtedly, players need to be motivated, so that they train hard and don't regard it as punishment. Enjoyment, therefore, is a factor which has to be considered, but I believe this can be attained through a variety of drills and practices, such as those found in this book, which are demanding and challenging, yet allow the players to express themselves when a ball is involved.

The aim of this book is to provide coaches, managers, teachers and parents with ideas to improve physical fitness combined with soccer skills, since ideally both should be developed together. However, the majority of players do not have access to ideal facilities or equipment during training, and inadequate playing surfaces often mean that ball work is limited or non-existent. For these players I have included a number of exercises which do not require a ball and can be carried out with poor lighting or playing surface. Many of the practices in this book have been collated over several years. However, quite a few have been devised or adapted by me and used in the many training sessions that I have run. I believe they will all improve fitness and some will improve technique, but above all, they will reduce monotony, which is a real danger when players train frequently. There is nothing worse than a loss of interest which leads to a desire by players to cut training short. I hope everybody who is involved in the training of players will find the practices in this book demanding yet worthwhile. In addition, I hope coaches adapt these ideas and are innovative themselves and look for new and sometimes unorthodox methods for training players, so that boredom and tedium do not become part of the vocabulary. It is vital that we attract youngsters to the game and keep them. To all coaches, I hope this book provides you with some new ideas and increases enjoyment.

SYMBOLS USED IN THIS BOOK

MOVEMENT OF THE PLAYER

MOVEMENT OF THE BALL

MOVEMENT OF THE PLAYER AND BALL

BACKWARD MOVEMENT OF THE PLAYER

SIDEWAYS MOVEMENT OF THE PLAYER

DRIBBLING MOVEMENT OF THE PLAYER

JOGGING/WALKING MOVEMENT OF THE PLAYER

JUMPING MOVEMENT OF THE PLAYER

CONE

M   MARKER

BALL

10M   DISTANCE

THE WARM UP

Before every training session or match, the coach should be strict about the warm up. Soccer players, like other athletes, often doubt the value of warming up and are keen to get on with the game or practice. For many, time is already too short for training, so fringe activities such as warm ups, mobility and stretching are often regarded as luxuries which can be done without. Coaches, therefore, have an important role to play and they themselves should have a basic understanding of the fundamentals of warming up and stretching. They are then in a position to impart this knowledge to the players and convince them of its value.

Why is it so important for players to warm up? Basically, it is an injury prevention measure, which allows players to adapt physically and mentally to the forthcoming exercise. Many injuries occur due to insufficient warm up. A cold muscle is relatively rigid and resilient to sudden increases in tension caused by rapid movements. When the elastic components of the muscle are unable to cope with the external tensions, the muscle will rupture. By warming up, players can therefore avoid injuries such as sprained ankles and 'pulled' muscles.

In addition to the physical effects, the warm up also has psychological benefits. Before a game it gives the player an opportunity to control his nerves, concentrate his thoughts and mentally rehearse the tasks he is about to perform. He should therefore be allowed to do the first part of the warm up on his own. However, it is important that a structured team warm up takes place because, left to their own devices, many players simply kick a ball to each other and neglect the jumps, turns and sprints that will soon become a part of the game.

What form should the warm up take? The exercise intensity should be low at the beginning and gradually increase. An inactive muscle has a low blood supply and a fairly low temperature. It takes approximately 10 to 15 minutes of intensive activity before the whole body reaches the necessary temperature. The best way to warm up, therefore, is to move so that the large muscles have to work. Jogging, running, jumping, heel kicks, skipping and so on, appear to be the best way of doing this, By the end of the warm up exercise intensity should be quite high, and at this point players can start to stretch.

When planning a warm up program, the coach should try to be creative. All the large muscle exercises should be performed with a ball. This will train technique, warm up the eyes, brain and feet and exercise the main muscle groups used for soccer. In addition, it is likely to be far more effective in motivating the players.

The warm up before the game should continue until shortly before the start of the match. When exercise stops, the temperature of the previously activated muscles decreases quickly and is back to pre-exercise level after about fifteen minutes, at which point the benefits gained from the warm up are lost. A considerable loss in temperature is also likely to occur at half-time, so it is advisable for players to perform some light activities before the start of the second half.

GENERAL WARM UP

The general warm up can be performed both individually and in groups and should last for 5 to 10 minutes. The following exercises can be used as part of this warm up and are ones with which most players are familiar. They can be performed across the pitch or around the outside.

1. Walking
2. Walking with long strides
3. Walking on the toes
4. Walking on the heels
5. Walking on the outer and inner edges of the feet
6. Walking with knees raised high
7. Walking with heels raised high
8. Jogging
9. Jogging with change of pace (speed up and slow down)
10. Jogging with heels touching the backside
11. Jogging with knees raised high
12. Grapevines (running sideways, right foot in front, than behind)
13. Jogging sideways, right foot leading, then left
14. Jogging, right hand touching the ground, left hand, then both hands
15. Jogging, with half-turns to the right and left
16. Jogging, drive off the right foot, then the left
17. Jogging, then jump up to head a ball
18. Jogging, jump up to head a ball, then put in a sharp run over 5 yards
19. Jogging backwards
20. Skipping, with knees touching, outstretched hands
21. Running with short, rapid strides
22. Running with extended strides
23. Running with a cadence of their own choice, alternating short and long strides (e.g. 10 long strides, followed by 10 short but quick ones)
24. Slow running forward, quick running backwards (e.g. 10 steps running forward, 6 steps running backwards quickly)
25. Jogging, two-footed jump forwards, followed by a sharp run over 5 yards
26. Jogging, hop several times on right or left foot, followed by a sharp run over 5 yards
27. Jog backwards, turn and run quickly over 5 yards
28. Jogging, both hands touch the ground, followed by a sharp run over 5 yards

WARM UP   PRACTICE 1

1. 6 markers are placed as in the diagram, with the 2 central markers (M1 and M2) approximately 20 yards apart.
2. The players line up in pairs and in 2 lines, either side of M1
3. The first pair start together and do the same movement down the center lane.
4. The whole group follows down the central lane, copying the first pair.
5. When they reach M2, the pairs break away and jog down their sidelines.
6. The movement down the center lane could include running sideways, backwards, heels to backside, high knees, skipping, grapevines, etc. The coach will inform the leading pair what the movement is going to be.
7. It is important to keep the players moving throughout the entire activity. Once the first pair have reached a third of the way down the center lane, the next pair should start.

WARM UP   **PRACTICE 2**

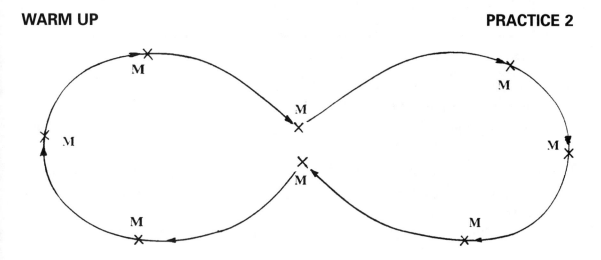

1. 8 markers are placed in a figure-8 pattern, as in the diagram. Any number of people can participate.
2. Players move around the cones performing exercises, which the coach calls out.
3. Movements could include jogging, running sideways, running with a change of pace, running backwards, running with the heels to the backside, skipping, touching the ground with hands, jumping to the head a ball, etc.
4. The direction should be changed regularly.
5. Make sure the course is big enough so that the players keep moving throughout the entire activity.

WARM UP   **PRACTICE 3**

$$X^1 \ X^2 \ X^3 \ X^4 \ X^5 \ X^6$$
$$Y^1 \ Y^2 \ Y^3 \ Y^4 \ Y^5 \ Y^6$$

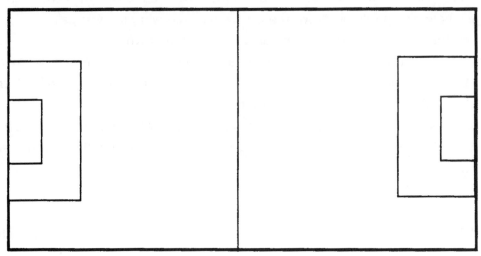

1. Any number of players form 2 lines and jog around the outside of the pitch. The lines should be 3 to 5 yards apart.
2. While moving around the pitch, the players perform exercises, which the coach calls out.
3. Movements could include jogging, running sideways, running backwards, running with heels to backside, skipping, touching the ground with both hands, jumping to head a ball, etc.
4. On a signal from the coach, the last pair race to the front, or the front pair race to the back.
5. Players should change direction regularly.

Variations
a) The 2 lines change places. It is important that those in the line moving from left to right (in this case Y's) go in front and those moving from right to left (in this case X's) go behind.
b) Players jump to head a ball before changing sides.
c) Players touch the ground with both hands before changing sides.
d) Players run sideways, hop, do two-footed jumps, grapevines, etc. to change sides.

WARM UP   **PRACTICE 4**

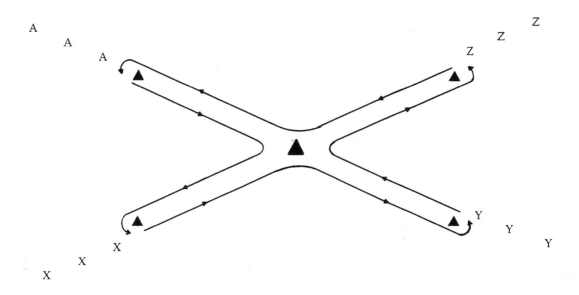

1. 4 cones are placed in a star shape, with 1 large cone in the middle. The players line up on the right-hand side of the 4 markers.
2. The distance from the markers to the middle is approximately 20 yards.
3. Each line jogs to the middle, turns and jogs to the marker on their right.
4. This process continues until the lines arrive back where they started.
5. Players now jog to the middle, but perform various warm up exercises on the way out to the cones.
6. These exercises can consist of jogging with a change of pace, running backwards, running sideways, grapevines, running with heels to backside, skipping, touching the ground with both hands, etc.

WARM UP   **PRACTICE 5**

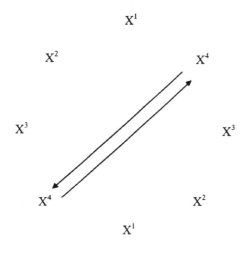

1. Players pair off and line up opposite each other in a circle.
2. When the coach shouts out a number, e.g. 4, both 4s run across and change places.
3. While running, players perform the usual warm up routines, such as running sideways, running backwards, skipping, accelerating and decelerating, etc.

Variations

a) The coach calls out more than one number, so that players have to avoid each other.
b) Players sprint, aiming to get across before their partner. The sprint could be preceded by jumps to head a ball, tuck jumps, etc.
c) 2 players enter the circle and 1 chases the other. If a player gets caught, he becomes the chaser. See who manages to catch the most in 35 seconds.

WARM UP   **PRACTICE 6**

X	Y	Z
X	Y	Z
X	Y	Z
X	Y	Z
X	Y	Z
(1)	(2)	(3)

1. Players line up in 3 lines. Each line is given a number.
2. Players perform the usual warm up routines, such as jogging, two-footed jumps, running with heels to backside, skipping, sprinting, etc. but on the spot.
3. When the coach calls out 2 numbers, the groups shuffle across quickly to change places, e.g. he might shout out 1/2. 1's quickly change places with 2's, but now assume 2's number and vice versa.

Variations

a) The same practice could be used, but on the move.
b) Players jump in the air and face the other way. The central line now has to be alive to the situation.

GENERAL WARM UP (INDEPENDENT) (A)   PRACTICE 7

Players will need a worksheet and can work independently or in twos or threes. Participants will follow the guidelines below and the warm up should take about 10 minutes to complete.

WARM UP

1. Travel around the area performing low-intensity activities to raise the pulse gradually.
2. Perform exercises on the spot to mobilize the hip and ankle joints in a controlled way.
3. Travel anywhere in the area and, at the same time, perform exercises to mobilize the shoulder and wrist joints.
4. Perform exercises on-the-spot to mobilize the different parts of the spine (neck, upper back, lower back).
5. Travel around the area performing a mixture of high and low impact activities. Keep the intensity moderate.
6. Perform stretches for the calf (gastrocnemius), chest (pectorals), and the back of the arm (triceps).
7. Perform actions on-the-spot, which will raise the pulse.
8. Perform stretches for the front of the upper leg (quadriceps), back of upper leg (hamstrings) and top of leg to pelvis (hip flexors). Hold each stretch for 10 seconds.
9. Travel around the area performing high impact (moderate to high intensity) activities. Use as much of the area as possible.
10. Perform stretches for the groin (insides of the upper leg or adductors) and the side muscles (obliques). Hold each stretch for 10 seconds
11. Shake out arms and legs, ready for action.

Diagrams showing the various stretches could be placed on the back of the worksheet, in order to make it easier for the players.

GENERAL WARM UP (INDEPENDENT) (B)   PRACTICE 8

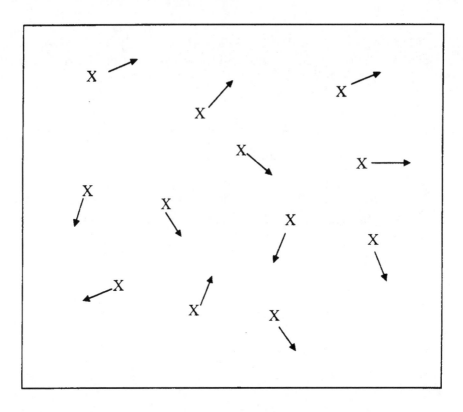

1. The players work in a square approximately 20 yards by 20 yards and any number can take part.
2. The coach will gradually build up a whole range of warm up activities, but the players will choose in what order they perform them.

THE WARM UP

a) The players jog anywhere they like in the area, but when they see a space they make a fast run into it.
b) As above, but the coach adds running backwards and running sideways.
c) As above, but the coach adds skipping and running with heels to backside.
d) As above, but the coach adds jogging with half-turns and drives from the ankle.
e) As above, but the coach adds running with a change of pace.

Any number of activities could be added to this list. The advantage of using this approach, in a confined space, is that players have to be aware of other people and it is they who decide when to use the various activities.

SPECIFIC WARM UP

Once players have performed the general warm up, which should have activated the large muscle groups, the process should continue with exercises for the main muscle groups used for soccer. For this it makes sense to use a ball, so that players can continue to warm up their eyes, brain and feet, as well as their muscles.

WARM UP   PRACTICE 1

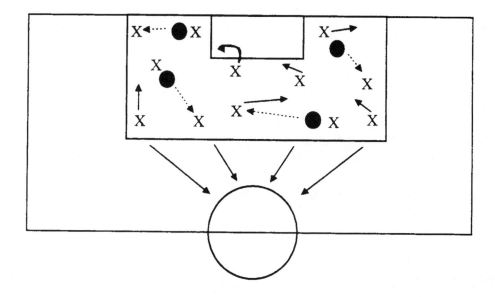

1. 4 balls are required for 12 players.
2. The players start in one penalty area and pass the balls first time amongst themselves. The players must keep moving at all times.
3. On a signal from the coach, the players run to another part of the field and continue to pass the ball in this area, e.g. the center circle.
4. On the next signal, the coach might move the players to the right touch line and on the next , back to the penalty area, and so on.
5. Passing can be replaced by alternatives, such as dribbling with cross-overs.

The following exercises, from No. 2 to No. 21, can follow the same pattern as Practice 1. The players perform the designated exercise, but on a signal from the coach, they run to another part of the field, where the practice continues.
The exercises can also be used for technical training or as part of the specific warm up, if the coach wishes.

WARM UP **PRACTICE 2**

1. 2 players stand facing each other at a distance of 3 to 4 yards. There is one ball.
2. The players pass the ball first time with the inside of the foot.
3. The coach must ensure that the players make the correct shape.

WARM UP **PRACTICE 3**

1. 2 players stand face-to-face about 8 yards apart.
2. X1 plays the ball along the ground to X2, who returns the ball first time with a chipped pass.
3. To turn the chip into the low pass, X1 can allow the ball to bounce once.
4. Change roles regularly.

WARM UP **PRACTICE 4**

1. 2 players stand facing each other about 4 to 5 yards apart.
2. On receiving the ball, each player must control the ball with one foot and pass back with the other.
3. Do not allow players to control and pass with same foot.

WARM UP **PRACTICE 5**

1. 2 players stand facing each other about 3 to 4 yards apart.
2. They pass the ball first time, but with the right foot only, so the ball has to be played at a slight angle.
3. Change to passing with the left foot only.

WARM UP   **PRACTICE 6**

1. 2 players stand facing each other about 4 to 5 yards apart.
2. X1 passes to X2, who drops his left shoulder before receiving the ball with his right foot.
3. He then touches the ball to the side, with the outside of his right foot and plays the ball back to X1 who repeats the maneuver.

Variation
Players drop their right shoulders before receiving the ball, touch the ball to the side with the outside of their left foot and pass back to their partners.

WARM UP   **PRACTICE 7**

1. 2 players stand facing each other about 10 yards apart and pass the ball first time.
2. Gradually they move closer together, still passing the ball, until they are less than a meter apart.
3. They hold this position for a few seconds, then gradually move away until they are back in their original positions.

WARM UP   **PRACTICE 8**

1. 2 players stand facing each other about 10 yards apart.
2. The players pass to each other first time, but X1 remains stationary and X2 gradually moves closer to him.
3. When X2 gets less than a meter away from X1, he holds this position for a few seconds, then slowly moves away until he resumes his original position.
4. Repeat with X2 remaining stationary and X1 moving in.

WARM UP

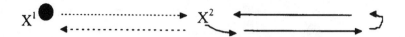

1. X1 has possession of a ball about 10 yards away from X2.
2. X2 turns and jogs slowly away from X1 and when he is ready he checks, turns quickly and sprints towards X1, calling for the ball at the same time.
3. X1 delivers the ball immediately on the call and X2 plays it back first time.
4. Repeat several times then reverse the roles.

WARM UP

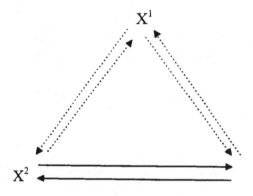

1. X1 has the ball and sends alternate passes to the left and right, which X2 has to return as quickly as possible.
2. X2 remains stationary.
3. Repeat several times then reverse the roles.

WARM UP

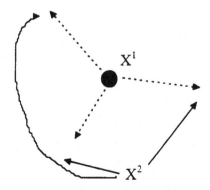

1. X1 has a ball and dispatches it in various directions, but no more than 10 yards away from him.
2. X2 has to retrieve the ball and pass it back to X1 as quickly as possible.

3. The serving player can also pick up the ball and demand other skills such as heading and volleying.
4. After 2 minutes the roles should be reversed.

WARM UP **PRACTICE 12**

a)

b)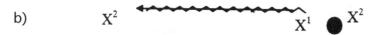

1. X1 and X2 stand facing each other about 12 yards apart.
2. X1 dribbles towards X2 and quickly follows his pass, so that he is standing in front of X2.
3. X2 controls the ball, dribbles around X1, then dribbles quickly to take up X1's original position.
4. The practice continues with X2 playing the ball to X1 and following his pass.

WARM UP **PRACTICE 13**

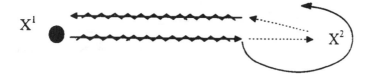

1. X1 and X2 stand facing each other about 15 yards apart. X1 has the ball.
2. X1 dribbles towards X2 and when he gets about 5 yards away, passes to him.
3. He then speeds up and sprints around X2 who plays the ball into his path.
4. X1 dribbles back to his starting position, passes the ball to X2 and the roles are reversed.

WARM UP **PRACTICE 14**

1. X1 and X2 stand facing each other about 1 yard apart. X1 has a ball and X2 stands with his legs apart.
2. X1 plays the ball through X2's legs, who turns and chases the ball.
3. X1 follows X2, so that he is just behind when X2 stops the ball.
4. The roles are now reversed. X1 stands with his legs apart, X2 plays the ball between them and the maneuver continues.

WARM UP   **PRACTICE 15**

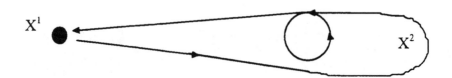

1. X1 and X2 stand facing each other about 12 yards apart.
2. X1 dribbles the ball with a change of tempo, around X2 and back to his place. On the way back he has to perform a trick with the ball.
3. While X1 is dribbling, X2 performs warm up exercises on the spot, e.g. two-footed jumps, jogging, running with heels to backside, skipping, etc.
4. When he gets back to his original position, X1 passes to X2 and the roles are reversed.

WARM UP   **PRACTICE 16**

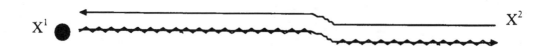

1. X1 and X2 stand facing each other about 10 yards apart.
2. X1 has a ball and dribbles to X2's spot. X2 runs to X1's spot.
3. When the players meet in the middle, both drop their left shoulders and pass each other on their right.
4. X1 passes to X2 and the process continues.

Variation
Players drop their right shoulder and go to the left.

WARM UP   **PRACTICE 17**

1. 2 players stand facing each other about 12 to 15 yards apart.
2. X1 passes to X2, who has to keep the ball off the ground, using any part of his body apart from his hands.
3. At the same time X1 runs around X2 and back to his place.
4. At this point X2 plays the ball to X1, who keeps the ball up without using his hands. Meanwhile X2 runs around his partner and back to his place.
5. While running the players can perform the usual warm ups such as skipping, running sideways, running with a change of pace, running backwards, etc.

Variation
Instead of passing the ball, players can head it back.

WARM UP   **PRACTICE 18**

1. 2 players stand facing each other about 4 yards apart. X1 has a ball.
2. X1 passes to X2, quickly shuffles 2 yards to his left and back to his place.
3. As soon as he recovers his position, X2 returns the ball to him and repeats the same movement.
4. It is important the ball is not passed back until players have recovered their starting position.

Variations
a) Players pass the ball then shuffle quickly to their right.
b) Players pass the ball, shuffle quickly forwards and back to their place.
c) Players pass the ball, shuffle quickly backwards then return to their place.
d) After passing the ball, players could jump in the air or touch the ground with both hands before starting the shuffle.

WARM UP   **PRACTICE 19**

1. 2 players line up about 5 yards apart. X1 has a ball.
2. X1 passes to X2 who controls the ball with the outside of his foot, dribbles 2 yards to his left, passes back to X1 and recovers his position.
3. X1 controls the ball with the outside of his foot, dribbles 2 yards to his left, passes back to X2 and recovers his position.

Variations
a) Players control the ball with the outside of the foot, dribble 2 yards to the right and pass back to their partners.
b) Players control the ball, dribble forwards 2 yards, pass and recover their position.
c) Players control the ball, dribble backwards 2 yards using the sole of the foot, pass and recover their position.

WARM UP   **PRACTICE 20**

X^1 X^2

1. 2 players stand facing each other about 15 yards apart.
2. X1 has the ball and X2 runs towards him at a moderate pace.
3. When X2 is about 7 yards from X1, X1 passes to X2, who returns it immediately and continues running forward.
4. X1 now rolls the ball past X2, who is still running towards him.
5. X2 now makes a half-turn, runs after the ball, stops it with the sole of his foot and turns around.
6. The process is repeated, but with X1 doing the running and X2 remaining stationary.

WARM UP   **PRACTICE 21**

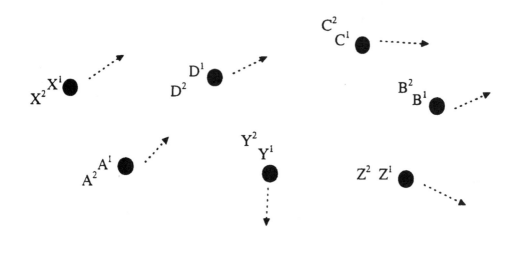

1. Players line up in pairs in a designated area, with 1 ball between 2 players.
2. The No. 1s dribble anywhere they like in the area and the No. 2s follow closely, performing the usual warm up routines, such as skipping, running sideways, running with heels to backside, etc.
3. Those dribbling the ball should change directions frequently.
4. After a short time, players change roles.
5. Players must be aware of each other.

Variation
No. 2s follow the No. 1s and tell them when to change directions.

WARM UP   PRACTICE 22

1. Any number of pairs line up on the goal line, with a ball between 2.
2. X's start and dribble towards line B.
3. On a signal from the coach, the players change direction and dribble at a faster tempo towards line A.
4. The drill continues with the players changing direction on the coach's signal. Each time they dribble towards line A the tempo is increased.
5. After a set time the partners change roles.
6. The partner who is not working with the ball should carry out the normal warm up routines on the spot.

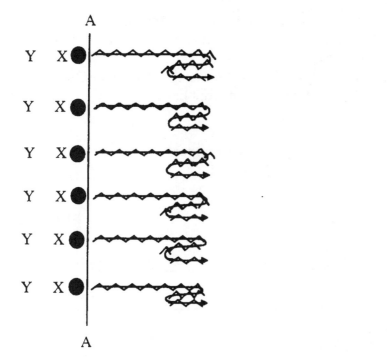

WARM UP   PRACTICE 23

1. 2 players stand about 20 yards apart. Each player has a ball.
2. Both players start dribbling towards each other at the same time.
3. When they are quite close, they pass the ball in the direction they are facing.
4. Both players then turn, run after the other player's ball, dribble it to the starting position and the exercise begins again.

WARM UP   PRACTICE 24

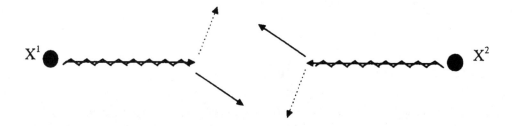

1. 2 players stand about 20 yards apart, each has a ball.
2. Both players start dribbling towards each other at the same time.
3. When they are quite close, they pass the ball to their left, then sprint to their right and collect their opponent's ball.
4. Both players then turn, face each other and the exercise starts again.
5. Make sure there is a change of tempo from the dribble to the chase.

Variation
Players pass to their right and sprint to collect their opponent's ball on the left.

WARM UP   PRACTICE 25

1. 2 players stand face-to-face about 20 yards apart.
2. X1 dribbles towards X2, who also starts for the center.
3. X1 passes on the run towards X2 when they are about 4 yards away.
4. After passing the ball X1 runs to X2's position and X2 dribbles to X1's position.
5. Both players then turn around and begin the exercise again.

WARM UP   **PRACTICE 26**

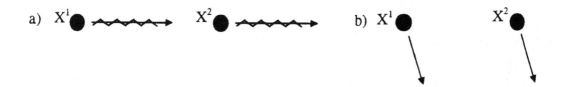

1. X1 and X2 have a ball each. X1 stands about 4 yards behind X2.
2. Both players dribble across the pitch. X1 has to track X2. If X2 speeds up, slows down, checks, etc. then X1 has to do the same.
3. Players change roles frequently.

Variations
a) X2 puts his foot on the ball and turns to collect his partner's ball. X1 immediately runs forward to take X2's ball.
b) The players dribble side-by-side, with the player on the left always being in control. If X2 speeds up, slows down, checks, etc. then X1 does the same.
c) The players dribble side-by-side. If X2 puts his foot on the ball, then X1 has to do the same. They immediately sprint across and take each other's ball and the exercise continues.

WARM UP   **PRACTICE 27**

1. 2 players stand facing each other about 4 yards apart. X1 has the ball.
2. X1 passes to X2, who stops the ball but keeps jogging backwards.
3. X1 runs forward, plays the stationary ball to X2 again and the process is repeated.
4. Change roles after working the width of the pitch.

Variations
a) X1 throws the ball for X2 to head back. After heading, X2 continues to jog backwards and the exercise is repeated.
b) X1 throws the ball for X2 to volley back. After volleying, X2 continues to jog backwards and the exercise is repeated

c) X1 plays the ball to X2, who jumps up and allows the ball to roll under his feet. As he lands he turns around, runs after the ball, stops it, turns around again and continues running backwards. X1 follows up, plays the ball again and the exercise is repeated.

WARM UP   PRACTICE 28

1. X1 and X2 stand facing each other about 5 yards apart.
2. They pass the ball to each other, but after each pass, jump in the air as if heading a ball.

Variations
a) After each pass, the players touch the ground with both hands.
b) After each pass, the players make a half-turn to the side and back again.
c) After each pass, the players squat then stand up again.

WARM UP   PRACTICE 29

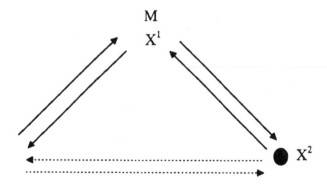

1. Players stand as in the diagram. X2 starts with the ball.
2. He plays a square ball into the open space in front of him, then sprints to X1's position.
3. X1 runs to the ball, passes to where X2 started and sprints back to the marker.
4. Meanwhile X2 runs back to his original position to take the return pass.
5. The exercise continues without interruption
6. A marker should be placed at X1's position.

WARM UP **PRACTICE 30**

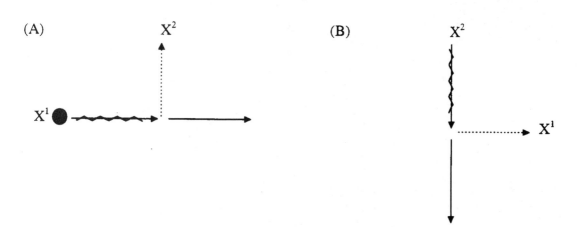

1. X1 and X2 take up positions as in diagram A. X1 has a ball.
2. X1 dribbles across and when level with X2, passes to him then speeds up for 5 yards.
3. X2, in turn, dribbles across and when level with X1, passes to him then speeds up for 5 yards.
4. This process is continuous.

Variations
a) After passing the ball, players can perform the usual warm up routines, such as running sideways, backwards, etc.
b) X2 takes up a position on X1's right. X1 now has to pass with his left foot.

WARM UP **PRACTICE 31**

1. Players take up positions in 3 corners of a square. The fourth corner is left free. X1 has a ball.
2. X1 passes to X2, then sprints for the free corner.
3. X2 passes to X3 and sprints for the free corner.
4. The process is continuous. Encourage players to pass first time.

Variation
Instead of running to the free corner, players can perform the usual warm up routines.

WARM UP   **PRACTICE 32**

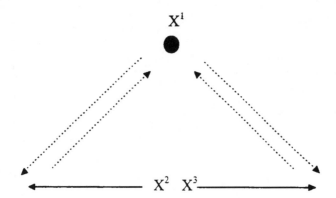

1. 3 players take up positions as in the diagram.
2. X1 has a ball and passes it once to his right, which X2 runs to collect and return, and once to his left, which X3 has to collect and return.
3. The process continues without interruption.
4. Players change roles regularly.

Variations
a) The chasing players have their backs to the server.
b) The server calls out the name of the player, who has to return it. Thus a player might have to collect it from the right or left.

WARM UP   **PRACTICE 33**

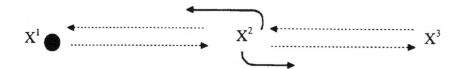

1. Passing among 3 players using one ball
2. X1 plays the ball to X2, who has one touch to turn and pass to X3.
3. X3 passes back to X2 and the process is repeated.
4. Make sure the player in the middle turns both ways.
5. Change roles regularly.

WARM UP   **PRACTICE 34**

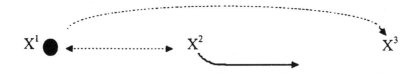

1. Chipping practice in 3s. The outside players are about 30 yards apart.
2. X1 plays the ball to X2 who comes to meet it and plays it back first time. X1 now chips the ball over X2, onto the feet or chest of X3.
3. X3 controls the ball, plays it to X2, gets the return and chips it first time to X1.
4. The process continues.

WARM UP **PRACTICE 35**

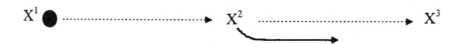

1. Chipping and volleying practice in threes. The outside players are 20 yards apart.
2. X1 chips the ball to X2, who has to control the ball without it touching the ground, turn and volley it to X3.
3. X3 then chips the ball to X2 and the process continues.

WARM UP **PRACTICE 36**

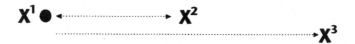

1. 2 players pass the ball through the legs of the middle man. The outside players are no more than 4 yards apart.
2. X1 plays the ball to X2, who returns it first time. X1 then plays the ball back, through the legs of X2 to X3.
3. X2 turns quickly, X3 plays the ball to him, gets the return, then plays the ball through the legs of X2 to X1 and the process is repeated.

WARM UP **PRACTICE 37**

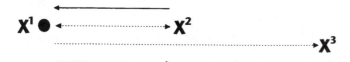

1. 2 players pass the ball through the legs of the middle man, but this time the players change places.
2. X1 plays the ball to X2 who returns it first time. X1 then plays the ball through X2's legs and changes places with him.
3. X3 then plays the ball to X1, who returns it first time. X3 then plays the ball through X1's legs and changes places with him.
4. X3 is now in the middle and the process is repeated.

WARM UP   **PRACTICE 38**

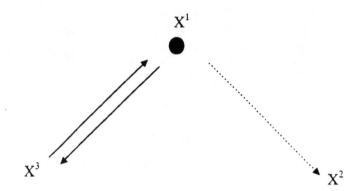

1. Changing positions in groups of 3. The players stand at the corners of a triangle.
2. X1 passes the ball to X2 and changes places with X3.
3. X2 then passes to one of the other players, and changes places with the free man.

WARM UP   **PRACTICE 39**

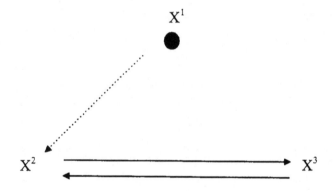

1. The players stand at the corners of a triangle. X1 has a ball.
2. X1 passes to either of the other players (in this case X2), but stays where he is.
3. X2, for whom the pass is intended, does not take it, but runs to the position of X3.
4. X3 in turn runs across to take the pass.
5. He then passes to either of the other players, and the process continues.

WARM UP   PRACTICE 40

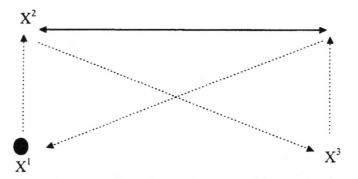

1. The players line up as in the diagram. X1 and X3 are 10 yards apart.
2. X1 plays a square ball to X2, who passes first time to X3.
3. As soon as he has played the ball, X2 sprints to collect a square pass from X3.
4. He turns quickly, plays the ball to X1 and the process starts again.
5. Positions should be changed at regular intervals.

WARM UP   PRACTICE 41

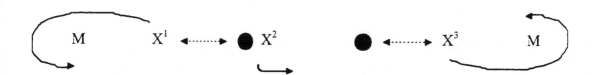

1. Players stand as in the diagram. The player in the middle has two balls. 2 markers are placed 10 yards behind X1 and X3.
2. X2 plays the ball backwards and forwards to X1. When X2 stops the ball, X1 turns to his left, sprints around the marker behind him and back to his place.
3. X2 immediately turns, sprints to the ball behind him and plays a 1/2 with X3. As soon as X2 puts his foot on the ball, X2 turns to his left, sprints around the marker behind him and back to his place.
4. The practice continues. Change the central players regularly.

Variations
a) The outside players turn to their right before sprinting around the marker.
b) The players jump to head a ball before sprinting around the marker.
c) The players touch the ground with both hands before sprinting around the marker.
d) The players run backwards around the marker.
e) The players sprint forwards around the marker in front of them and join the back of the opposite line, i.e. X1 will take X3's position.
f) To make the practice less demanding, 5 players can be used instead of 3.

WARM UP **PRACTICE 42**

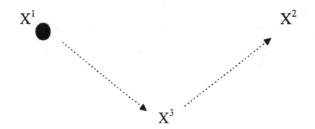

1. Passing among 3 players.
2. X1 passes to X3, who returns the ball first time to X2.
3. X2 returns the ball first time to X3 who plays it back to X1 and so on.
4. After some time the players change position.

Variations
a) X3 moves backwards during the practice. X1 and X2 move forwards.
b) X3 moves forwards and X1 and X2 move backwards.
c) After passing the ball, the players jump in the air or touch the ground with both hands.

WARM UP **PRACTICE 43**

1. 2 players start off 20-25 yards apart. Both have a ball.
2. They dribble slowly towards each other and when they are about 2 yards apart, play their balls forward at the same time.
3. They immediately turn and sprint after the ball their partners have played.
4. They stop the ball, turn and repeat the exercise.
5. It is important that there is a change of tempo.

WARM UP **PRACTICE 44**

1. 2 players stand as in the diagram, about 10 yards apart. Both have a ball.
2. They start simultaneously, passing the ball with the instep, in the direction shown in the diagram.
3. X1 then runs for X2's ball and vice versa.
4. The exercise is then repeated in the opposite direction.
5. It is important that the players weight the pass according to the movement of their partner.

WARM UP   **PRACTICE 45**

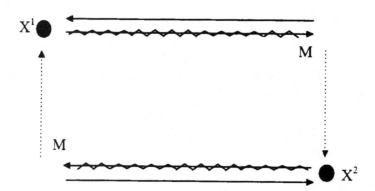

1. 2 players stand as in the diagram, about 10 yards apart. Both have a ball.
2. They start simultaneously, dribbling the ball slowly in the direction shown in the diagram.
3. On reaching the markers, they pass the ball to their partner's original position and sprint back to collect the other ball.
4. They stop the ball, turn and repeat the exercise.

WARM UP   **PRACTICE 46**

1. 2 players stand facing each other about 8 yards apart. X1 has 2 balls.
2. He passes the first one along the ground, which X2 returns first time.
3. He then throws the next one up in the air, which X2 has to jump up and head back.
4. The exercise is continued without interruption.
5. Change roles after a time.

WARM UP   PRACTICE 47

1. 2 players stand facing each other about 8 yards apart. X1 has the ball.
2. X1 throws the ball for X2 to jump up and head back.
3. After heading the ball, X2 has to quickly perform one push- up, then resume his standing position.
4. Repeat 15 times then change roles.

Variation
After performing the skill, e.g. passing, heading or volleying, other exercises such as sit ups, or squat jumps could be used.

WARM UP   PRACTICE 48

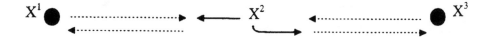

1. 3 players stand according to the diagram. X1 and X2 have a ball each.
2. X1 sends a short pass to X2, who runs to meet it and returns it first time.
3. At that point X3 sends a short pass to X2, who makes a quick half-turn, runs towards the ball and passes back to X3.
4. The drill continues.
5. Make sure the passes are weighted so that X2 has to run towards the ball.

Variation
X1 plays the ball for X2 to pass back, but X2 then turns and heads back the next ball from X3. Volleys could be used instead of passes or headers.

WARM UP   PRACTICE 49

1. 2 players stand facing each other about 4 yards apart. Each has a ball.
2. They start passing to each other at the same time.
3. To avoid collisions, it is easier if both players pass the first ball with their right foot and the second with their left.

WARM UP   **PRACTICE 50**

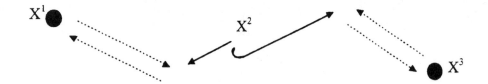

1. Passing among 3 players using 2 balls. The middle player dictates the practice!
2. X1 has the ball and X2 tells him where he wants the ball played.
3. X2 plays the ball back first time, turns quickly and demands the next ball from X3.
4. Repeat for approximately one minute, then change roles.

WARM UP   **PRACTICE 51**

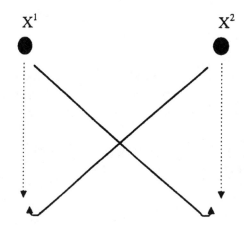

1. 2 players stand as in the diagram. Each has a ball.
2. Simultaneously they pass their ball in a parallel direction.
3. They then sprint after each other's ball by crossing one another's path.
4. They stop the balls, turn and pass in the opposite direction, along the same paths.
5. The exercise starts again

WARM UP **PRACTICE 52**

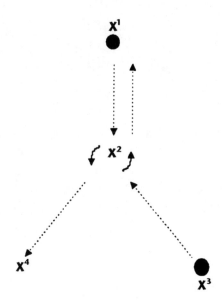

1. In 4s, passing to the player without a ball. X1 and X3 have a ball each.
2. X1 plays his ball to X2. He turns sharply and lays it off to the spare player (X4).
3. As soon as he has done that, X3 plays his ball to X2 who lays it off to the spare player (X1).
4. Quick reactions are required by the central player. Work him for a given length of time then change the roles.

WARM UP **PRACTICE 53**

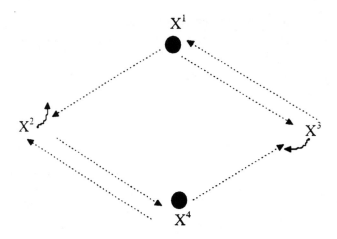

1. Passing to central players using 2 balls.
2. X1 plays a ball to X3, who returns it first time.

3. Simultaneously X4 plays a ball to X2, who also returns it first time.
4. Both central players then rotate quickly and X2 returns a ball played in by X4 and X2 a ball played in by X1.
5. The whole sequence is then repeated.
6. Change the central players regularly.

WARM UP **PRACTICE 54**

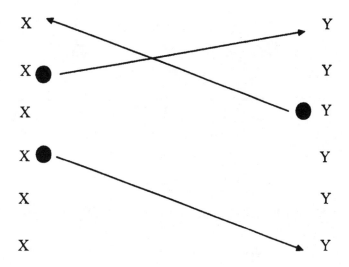

1. Players line up as in the diagram, about 20 yards apart. 3 balls for 12 players. With fewer players, the number of balls should be reduced.
2. On the command of the coach, those with the balls dribble across to players on the opposite side and take their place.
3. While dribbling, players must be aware of others, as well as their own ball.
4. It is important that players change tempo while dribbling.

Variations
a) Players dribble across, then pass to an unmarked teammate, making sure they call a name. After passing, players can perform the usual warm up drills, such as skipping, running sideways, heels to backside, etc.
b) Players pass and sprint after the ball.

WARM UP **PRACTICE 55**

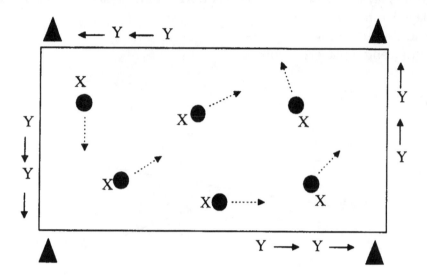

1. Players work in pairs. X's warm up with a ball in the square, while Y's warm up on the outside.
2. X's dribble where they like, but have to change tempo and find various ways of dribbling.
3. Y's perform the usual warm-up routines of jogging on the spot, two-footed jumps on the spot, running around the outside with heels to backside, sideways running, skipping, running backwards, jumping in the air, touching the ground with both hands, etc.
4. After a certain time the players change places, but before doing so have to play a 1/2 with their partners.

WARM UP **PRACTICE 56**

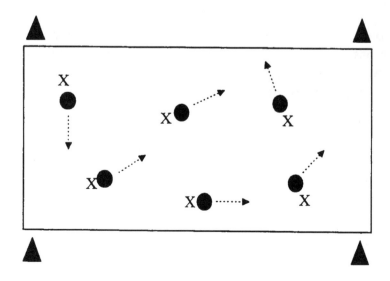

1. The players have a ball each and dribble where they like in the square.
2. However, when the coach puts up his right hand, the players have to stop the ball and carry out his instructions. (This makes the players dribble with their heads up.)
3. The instructions could include any of the following:
    a)   dragging the ball back with the sole of the foot
    b)   jumping backwards and forwards over the ball
    c)   feet on and off the top of the ball
    d)   astride jumps over the ball
    e)   run around the ball 6 times
    f)   jump from side-to-side over the ball
    g)   run on the spot with heels to backside
    h)   sprint on the spot for 5 seconds
4. Once the players have carried out the coach's instructions, they continue dribbling the ball with their heads up.

WARM UP   **PRACTICE 57**

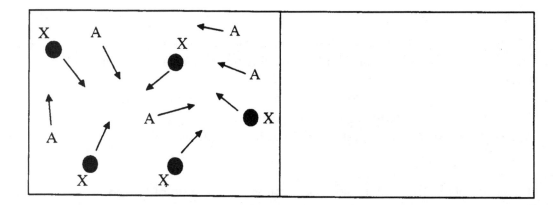

1. Players work in pairs. X's have a ball each.
2. A's run anywhere they like in the square AND have the right of way.
3. X's dribble where they like, but avoid A's.
4. A's perform the usual warm up routines, such as skipping, running sideways, running backwards, etc.
5. On a signal from the coach, all players sprint over to the other square, where they change roles.

Variations
a) A's stand still, but can move a couple of feet towards a man with a ball (but cannot tackle).
b) A's stand still, while X's dribble around as many players as possible. (Once they have been around a player, they cannot go around the same player until they have gone around another).
c) Players without a ball stand still with their legs open. Players with a ball pass it through their legs. However, they cannot return to that player until they have gone through the legs of someone else.

WARM UP   **PRACTICE 58**

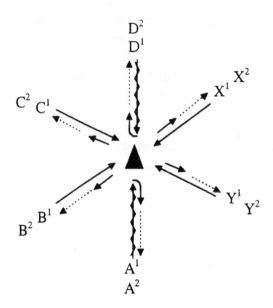

1. A circle is formed with a cone in the middle. Players work in pairs.
2. The first player in each pair dribbles to the middle, does a designated turn and passes the ball back to his partner.
3. On the way back he performs the usual warm ups, such as running backwards, sideways running, running with heels to backside, etc.
4. The second player does not start until his partner returns.

Variations
a) Players dribble to the middle and back, but with a change of tempo.
b) Players dribble to the middle, then play a 1/2 with their partner on the way back.
c) Players dribble to the middle and back, then dribble counter-clockwise around the circle. The partners, in the meantime, do continuous shuttles to the markers on their left, until the dribbler returns.
d) Players dribble to the middle and back, then dribble clockwise around the circle. The partners, in the meantime, do shuttles to the markers on their right, until the dribbler returns.

WARM UP PRACTICE 59

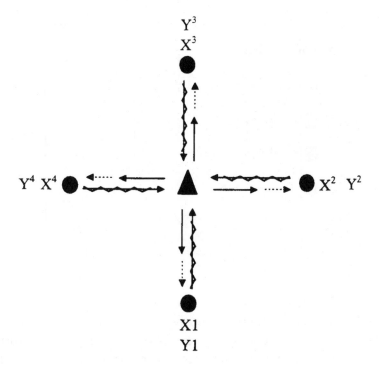

1. 8 players position themselves as in the diagram. A cone is placed in the middle. Each X player has a ball.
2. Simultaneously the X's dribble to the middle. At the cone they turn to their right, pass to the Y's and follow their pass.
3. Y's dribble to the middle, turn to their right, pass to the X's and follow their pass.
4. The coach stipulates the type of turn in the middle, e.g. inside of left foot, inside of right foot, outside of left foot, outside of right foot and sole of foot.
5. After passing the ball, players can perform the usual warm up routines, such as running backwards, running sideways, etc.

Variation
Players dribble to the middle, pass to their left and follow their pass.

WARM UP

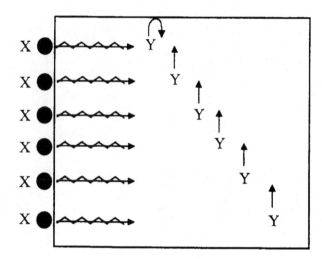

1. Players line up as in the diagram. X's have a ball each.
2. Y's set off at intervals and run continuously to an end line and back.
3. On the way they perform the usual warm up routines, such as running sideways, running backwards, running with half-turns, running with a change of tempo, etc.
4. X's, in the meantime, dribble across the area and back, but have to avoid the Y's, who have right of way.
5. Players work for 5 minutes, then change roles.

WARM UP

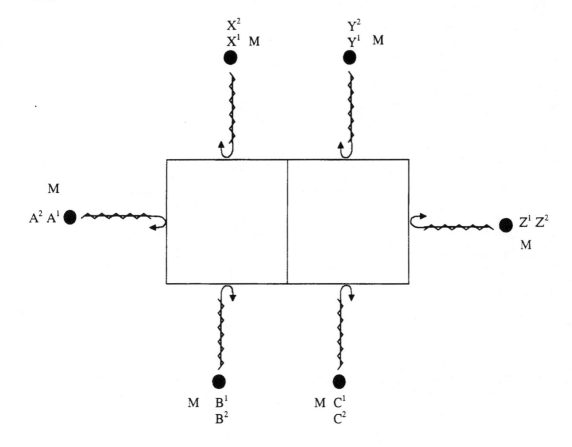

1. Players work in pairs. Each pair starts on a marker, 20 yards from one side of a 10 x 10 yard square.
2. The first player in each pair has a ball and dribbles to the line in front, and back to the marker. He changes the tempo throughout.
3. The second player follows a yard behind, performing the usual warm up routines, such as sideways running, running backwards, running with half-turns, etc.
4. The players change roles regularly.

Variations

a) One player acts as a defender and stands 4 yards from the line. He may retreat but not cross the line. The attacker starts 30 yards away and tries to beat the defender and take the ball into the square. After a certain time the players change roles.
b) X1 stands on the line with a ball and his partner faces him about 10 yards away. X1 passes to X2, then runs to touch the markers on his left and right. As he arrives back in the middle, X2 passes to him again, gets the return and the process starts again. After a certain time the players change roles.

WARM UP   PRACTICE 62

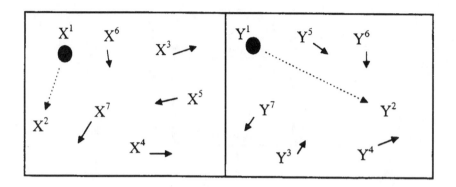

1. Any number of players line up in 2 squares. Each player is given a number.
2. Number 1 starts with the ball and passes to number 2, number 2 to number 3 and so on. The ball should be passed first time by more advanced players.
3. When the ball reaches the final man, it is passed back to number 1 and the sequence starts again.
4. When players do not have the ball, they should move freely about the area, performing the usual warm up routines, such as running sideways, running backwards, skipping, etc.
5. When players are confident in their passing, a second ball should be introduced, e.g. number 1 and number 6 start with a ball each and continue to pass in sequence.

Variations
a) After each pass, players perform certain tasks suggested by the coach. For example, they might put in a sprint, jump to head a ball, sprint on-the-spot, run backwards, etc.
b) Put one team in bibs, then open up the center grid line, so the groups are mixed. The sequence continues as before.

WARM UP   PRACTICE 63

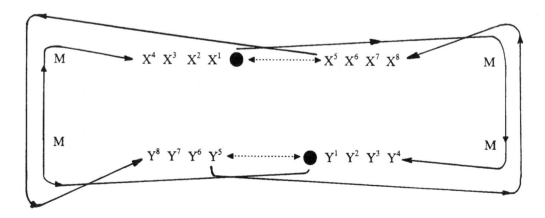

1. Players line up as in the diagram. The larger the group, the further away the markers should be.
2. X1 and Y1 have a ball each. Simultaneously they pass to the players opposite, then run around the markers to join the back of the appropriate line.
3. The balls are returned first time by X5 and Y5, who then run around the markers to the appropriate files
4. While running, players perform the usual warm up routines.
5. If there is nobody to pass to (and this sometimes happens) players must wait until someone arrives.

WARM UP   **PRACTICE 64**

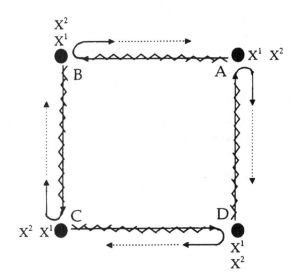 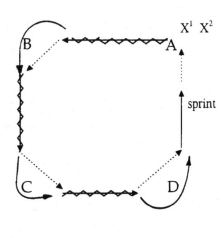

1. Players line up as in the diagram, in a 10 yard square. One ball per pair.
2. Number 1s start by dribbling to the marker opposite. Here they turn, pass to their partners and perform the usual warm up routines on the way back.
3. Number 2 repeats the process.

Variations
a) A 1/2 is played with the spare man at the marker in front, before turning quickly and passing back to the partner.
b) A 1/2 is played with the spare man at each marker.
c) Players dribble out and back, but change the tempo both ways.
d) Number 1and 2 dribble around the square, play the ball on the inside of the cone in front of them, then sprint around it to catch up with the ball. This is done at each cone. After the last, the ball is played to the partner and the player sprints home (see diagram B)

WARM UP   **PRACTICE 65**

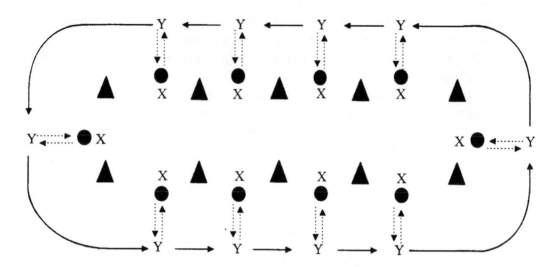

1. The X's line up between 2 cones, which are 8 yards apart. X's have a ball each and the Y's face them about 5 yards away.
2. On a signal from the coach, X's pass to the Y's, who return the ball first time.
3. Y's then move in a counter-clockwise direction, receiving a pass from each X in turn, until they are back at the point where they started.
4. X's and Y's then change roles.

Variations
a) Players move in a clockwise direction.
b) X's throw the ball for Y's to head back.
c) X's throw the ball for Y's to control on their chest and volley back.
d) X's throw the ball for Y's to half-volley back.
e) Players on the outside have 2 touches of the ball.
f) Players on the outside have 3 touches of the ball.

WARM UP   **PRACTICE 66**

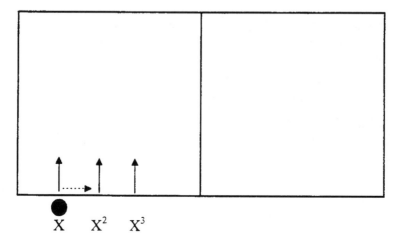

X X^2 X^3

1. Players are divided into groups of 3 or 4. One ball for each group.
2. The players jog from one side of the pitch to the other, passing the ball.
3. When receiving a pass or passing the ball, players run normally.
4. Those players not passing or receiving the ball perform the usual warm up routines, such as heels to backside, jumping to head a ball, running backwards, high knees, grapevines, etc.

WARM UP   **PRACTICE 67**

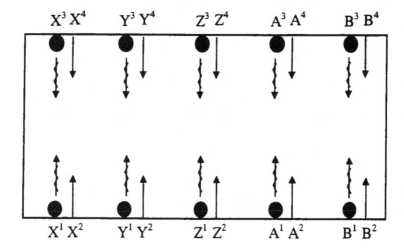

$$X^3\ X^4 \qquad Y^3\ Y^4 \qquad Z^3\ Z^4 \qquad A^3\ A^4 \qquad B^3\ B^4$$

$$X^1\ X^2 \qquad Y^1\ Y^2 \qquad Z^1\ Z^2 \qquad A^1\ A^2 \qquad B^1\ B^2$$

1. Players are divided into pairs with 1 ball for each pair. They line up as in the diagram.
2. The players jog from one side to the other, dribbling and passing the ball.
3. When not in possession of the ball, players perform the usual warm up routines.
4. On the way across, players must be aware of others coming in the opposite direction.
5. As players become more proficient, speed up the process and shorten the width of the pitch to no more than 25 yards. This will ensure that players are continually turning and avoiding players coming in the opposite direction.

WARM UP   **PRACTICE 68**

1. The A's form a large circle and have a ball each; the X's face them about 4 yards away.
2. On a signal from the coach, the A's pass their balls to the X's, who return them first time. They then run to any other A in the circle who is free and play a 1/2 with him.
3. They continue to do this for 40 seconds, then change roles.
4. The X's must be careful to avoid other players and be alert to where an A is free.

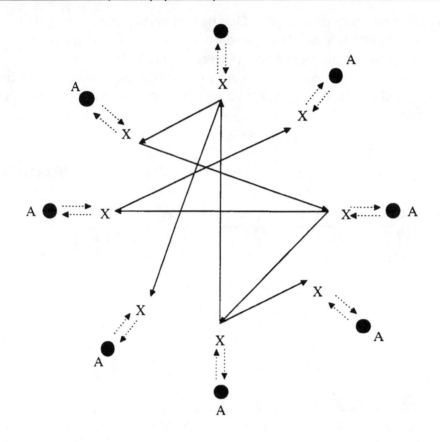

Variations

a) The working players have 2 touches.

b) A throws the ball for X to volley back.

c) The working players have 3 touches. They pass back on the third.

d) A throws the ball for X to half-volley back.

e) A throws the ball for X to head back.

f) A throws the ball for X to chest and volley back.

g) A throws the ball for X to knock up with one foot and volley back with the other.

WARM UP   **PRACTICE 69**

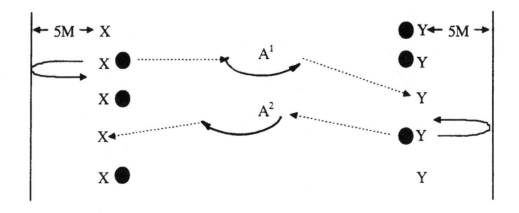

1. 2 rows of 5 players line up facing each other, 20 yards apart. Any 3 players in each row have a ball.
2. A1 calls for a ball from one of the X's and turns and passes to a free man in the Y's.
3. He then calls for a ball from one of the Y's, turns and passes to a free X.
4. A2 works to the opposite side.
5. Players on the outside, once they have passed the ball, sprint to a 5 yard line and back.

WARM UP   **PRACTICE 70**

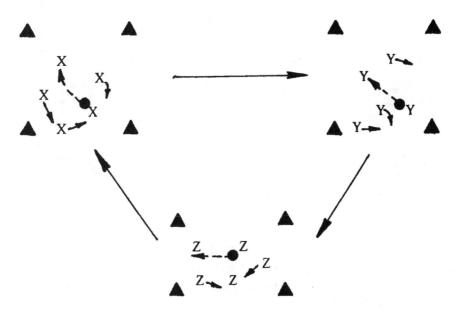

1. 3 15 yd. by 15 yd. grids are placed in one half of the pitch, approximately 40 yards apart. A group of 5, 6, or 7 players is in each grid.
2. X's, Y's and Z's have one ball per grid and pass and move in their own square. All the passing is first time and a player cannot pass back to the person who gave him the ball.
3. On a signal from the coach, the players leave their ball and run to the next grid, in a clockwise direction.
4. The above action is repeated after a pre-determined time.

Variations
a) Two touch
b) 3 touch
c) Players take the ball with the front foot
d) Players take the ball with the back foot.
e) Players control with the instep and pass with the outside of the foot.
f) Players control with the outside of the foot and pass with the instep.
g) 4 v 1 (The last player to get to the grid becomes the defender.)
h) Players call out who they are going to pass to before receiving the ball.
i) Players run in a counter-clockwise direction and take the ball with them.

WARM UP   **PRACTICE 71**

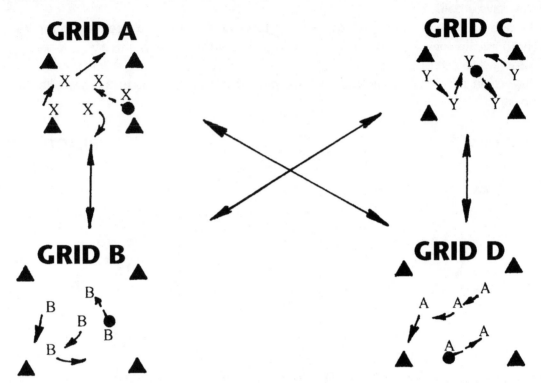

1. 4 15 yd. by 15 yd. grids are placed in one half of the pitch, approximately 30 yards apart. A group of 5, 6 or 7 players is in each grid.
2. X's, Y's, B's and A's have one ball per grid and pass and move in their own square. All the passing is first time.
3. On a signal from the coach, the players leave their ball and run to the facing grid. Thus grids A and B change places and grids C and D change places.
4. This action is repeated after a pre-determined time.

Variations
a) Grids change diagonally. Thus A changes with D and B changes with C.
b) Two touch
c) 3 touch
d) Players take the ball with the front foot.
e) Players take the ball with the back foot.
f) Players control with the inside of the foot and pass with the outside.
g) Players control with the outside of the foot and pass with the inside.
h) 4 v 1
i) Players play 1/2's then pass.

SUMMARY

1. The aim of the warm up is to prevent injury and allow players to adapt physically and mentally to the forthcoming exercise.
2. The exercise intensity should be low in the beginning and gradually increase.
3. It takes approximately 10 to 15 minutes before the body reaches the necessary temperature. The best way to ensure this happens is to exercise the large muscle groups.
4. By increasing the body temperature, nerves react faster and messages are carried more quickly from the brain to the muscles.
5. Soccer players use active flexibility during a game, so dynamic flexibility drills are more important than static flexibility prior to training or playing.
6. Before a game, players should be allowed to perform the first part of the warm up on their own. There should be a structured team warm up, which must include lots of work with a ball.
7. The warm up should continue as close as possible to the start of the match. This should prevent the temperature of activated muscles from returning to pre-exercise levels.
8. Some light activities should be performed at half-time in order to prevent a considerable loss in temperature.
9. The pre-training warm up does not need to be as intense as the pre-match warm up, since the coach can determine the intensity of the session.
10. The pre-training warm up must activate the large muscle groups and should mainly include work with the ball.
11. Players under 14 should not have to endure the normal warm up and stretching routines. This time can be better spent developing balance and co-ordination through fun games and activities.
12. The match or training session should conclude with a 15 minute warm down, as this will get rid of the waste products produced during the game and should consist of exercises such as light running, skipping and stretching.

GENERAL TRAINING DRILLS AND GAMES

The following general training drills provide material that will develop a feeling for the ball and improve a player's skill and technique. This basic skill development will include role skills such as passing, heading, ball control and dribbling. In addition to skill development, the coach can improve the physical fitness of his players by adapting the practices to suit any of the energy systems he wishes to train. Some of the exercises are quite complex, so it is up to the coach to decide which element of the practice is given priority. It is also important that players are told the purpose of the exercise and what the coach hopes to gain from it.

If the aim is to improve basic technique, then the drills should be introduced slowly, gradually speeding up as the performance improves and learning takes place. The coach should start with the simplest drills and then, when mastered, go on to the more complex ones and then variations. Whatever happens, the coach should not allow the drills to become monotonous and so a variety of them should be used. Nevertheless, players should practice until there is evidence of learning.

If the drills are to be used for speed training, then it is necessary to introduce longer intervals and greater recuperation, so the size of the groups should be increased where possible and the distance between players reduced. This will encourage the performers to make short but explosive bursts. Emphasis should be placed on acceleration and the strength of the first five steps.

If the coach wishes to improve endurance, then this can be emphasized strongly by reducing the size of the group and placing players further apart, thus increasing the length of the run or by putting markers down which have to be sprinted around, before rejoining the group. Spare players should also be available in order to keep momentum going, in case the practice breaks down. The drill should continue for between 3 and 6 minutes, then allow a minute for active recovery before recommencing.

If speed endurance is the target, then the players should remain some distance apart. Similarly, if players are working in a circle, this distance must stay large. The time while working should be restricted to between 30 and 45 seconds and players should be encouraged to work maximally when performing. Whatever the aim of the sessions, the advantage of using these exercises as part of the conditioning program is that, as well as improving fitness, other elements of the game such as technique and tactics can be trained at the same time. If conditioning is the main priority, then the coach must make sure the practice is set up correctly and that the exercise is completed in an intensive fashion. At the same time, it is also important that players pay attention to accuracy, touch and good performance.

GENERAL TRAINING DRILL   PRACTICE 1

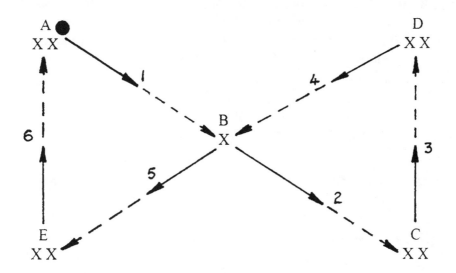

1. 1 player at B, 2 or more players at A, C, D, E. 1 ball at A.
2. A passes to B and follows his pass. The ball is then kicked in a figure-8 pattern as shown. B to C, C to D, D to B, B to E and E to A.

Variations
a) A second ball is introduced at C.
b) Players dribble the ball instead of pass.
c) Set up play. A passes to B, who sets up the ball for A to pass to C, A takes B's place. B sprints to C, who has set up the ball for A to pass to C, A takes B's place. B sprints to C, who has set up a ball to pass to D. The drill continues.

GENERAL TRAINING DRILL   PRACTICE 2

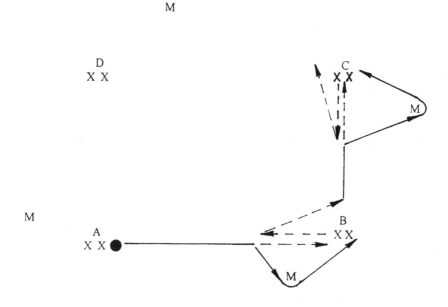

1. 2 or more players at A, B, C, D. One ball at A.
2. A passes to B, runs on and receives a return pass from B. B now breaks towards C. A passes to B and joins B after going around the marker.
3. B passes to C and takes a return from C. C breaks towards D. B passes to C and joins C after going around the marker.
4. The drill continues.

Variation
Use two balls, one starting at A and one at C.

GENERAL TRAINING DRILL   PRACTICE 3

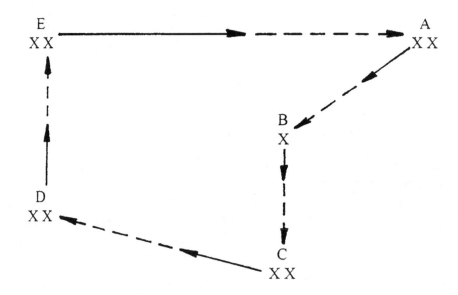

1. 2 or more players at A, B, C, D and E. 1 player at B, 1 ball at A.
2. A passes to B and follows his pass. B turns, passes to C and follows his pass. The drill continues in the path shown.

Variations
a) Introduce a second ball at D.
b) Dribble the ball instead of pass.
c) Set up play. A plays the ball to B and sprints after it. B sets up a ball for A to pass to C. A then takes B's place. B sprints to C, who has set up a ball for B to pass to D. The drill continues.

GENERAL TRAINING DRILL   PRACTICE 4

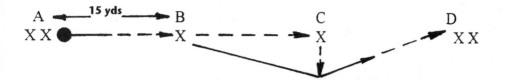

1. 2 or more players at A and D. 1 player at B and C. 1 ball at A.
2. A plays the ball to B and takes B's place.
3. B turns and passes to C, takes a return from C, passes to D and joins D.
4. D passes to C and joins C.
5. C turns and passes to B, takes a return from B and passes to A and joins A.
6. The drill continues.

Variation
To increase the fitness aspect of the drill, markers can be placed behind A and D, which the incoming players must run around before joining the back of their respective groups.

GENERAL TRAINING DRILL   PRACTICE 5

1. 2 or more players at A and D. 1 stationary player at C. 1 ball at B.
2. A runs to B, collects the ball and passes to C. He takes a return ball from C, passes to D and joins D.
3. D passes to C, takes a return pass, dribbles to B and leaves the ball. He then joins the back of A.
4. The drill continues.

Variation
To increase the fitness aspect of the drill, markers can be placed at the back of A and D, which the incoming players must run around before joining the back of their respective groups.

GENERAL TRAINING DRILL   PRACTICE 6

A   B   C   D

$X^3 \, X^2 \, X^1$ ●   ●

1. 3 or more players at A. 1 ball at B and C. 1 cone at D, 30 yards from A.
2. X1 collects the ball from C and replaces it at D. He collects the ball from B, replaces it at C and joins the back of A.
3. X2 picks up at C, replaces at B, then picks up at D, replaces at C and joins A.
4. The drill continues. This can be used as a relay competition between groups.

GENERAL TRAINING DRILL   PRACTICE 7

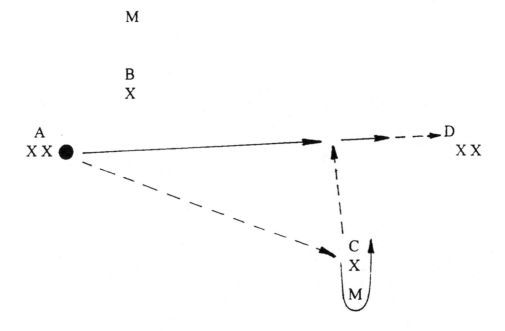

1. 2 or more players at A and D. 1 player at B and C.
2. A passes to C, gets a return ball, passes to D and joins D.
3. D passes to B, gets a return ball, passes to A and joins D.
4. The drill continues.

Variations
a) A passes to B and runs towards D. B passes to C, who returns the ball first time to A. A passes to D and joins D.
b) D passes to C and runs in the direction of A. C passes to B and B returns to D, who passes to A.
c) To make B and C more active, markers are placed behind them which they must run around once they have passed the ball.

GENERAL TRAINING DRILL **PRACTICE 8**

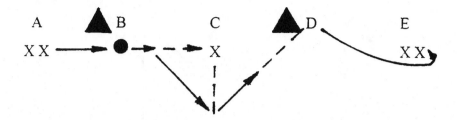

1. 2 or more players at A and E. 1 stationary player at C. Cones at B and D. 1 ball at B. Distance between A and E is 40 yards.
2. A sprints to B, collects the ball, passes to C, takes a return pass, dribbles to D where he leaves the ball and joins the back of E.
3. E returns, performing the same routine.

GENERAL TRAINING DRILL **PRACTICE 9**

1. 2 or more players at A and D, 1 at B and C. 1 ball at A.
2. A passes to C and sprints to B.
3. B turns, takes a short pass from C, passes to D and joins D.
4. D passes to B and sprints to C.
5. C turns, takes a short pass from B, passes to A and joins A.
6. The drill continues.

GENERAL TRAINING DRILL **PRACTICE 10**

1. 3 or more players at A and B. 1 ball at A, cones in front of A and B.
2. A plays a diagonal ball to B, sprints around the cone in front of him and joins the back of his group.
3. B returns the ball first time, sprints around the cone in front of him and joins the back of his group.
4. The drill continues.

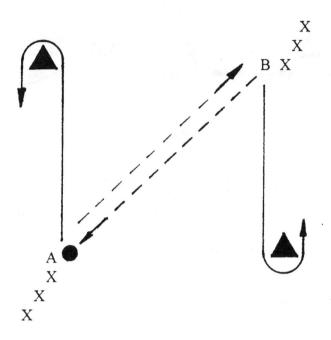

Variation
A plays the ball to B, runs around the cone in front of him and joins the back of B's group.

GENERAL TRAINING DRILL   **PRACTICE 11**

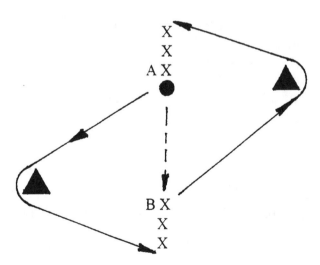

1. 2 or more players at A and B. 1 ball at A. 2 cones placed, as in the diagram.
2. A passes to B, sprints around the cone on his right and joins the back of B.
3. B returns the ball first time to A, runs around the cone on his right and joins the back of A.
4. The drill continues.

Variations

a) After playing the ball, the runners sprint around the cones on their left, just before joining the back of the opposite group.
b) To make the practice physically more demanding, markers could be placed at the back of each group which also must be run around.
c) The markers could be replaced with hurdles.

GENERAL TRAINING DRILL   PRACTICE 12

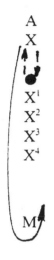
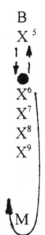

1. 4 or more players line up in a row, with another player facing them at a distance of 5 yards. A marker is placed several yards behind the line of players. X1 and X6 start with a ball.
2. X1 plays the ball to X, turns outside, sprints around the marker and joins the back of his line.
3. X6 plays the ball to X5, turns outside, sprints around the marker and joins the back of his line.
4. X and X5 immediately pass to the next player in line and the drill continues.
5. Change the face-up player regularly.

Variations

a) After passing the ball, the players turn inside, sprint around the marker and join the back of the group.
b) After passing the ball, the players turn outside, sprint around both markers and join the back of the opposite group.

NB: To increase the fitness aspect of the exercise, the markers can be placed further apart.

GENERAL TRAINING DRILL   **PRACTICE 13**

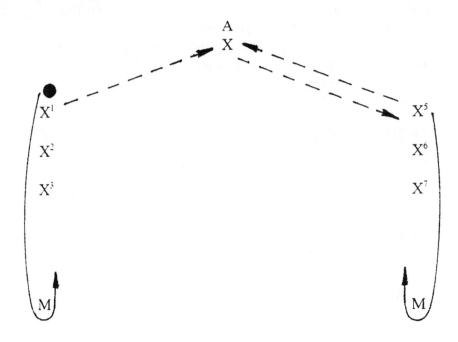

1. Players line up in two rows, with 3 or more in each. Another player faces the group 5 yards away. X1 starts with the ball.
2. X1 plays the ball to X, turns outside, sprints around the marker and joins the back of the line.
3. X plays the ball to X5, who returns it first time, then turns outside, sprints around the marker and joins the back of the line.
4. The drill continues. Change the face-up player regularly.

Variations
a) After passing the ball, the players turn inside, sprint around the marker and join the back of the line.
b) After passing the ball, the players turn outside, sprint around both markers and join the back of the opposite line.
c) After passing the ball, the players turn inside and sprint to the back of the opposite line.

NB: To increase the fitness aspect of the exercise, place the markers further back.

GENERAL TRAINING DRILL   **PRACTICE 14**

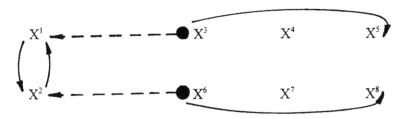

1. Players form 2 lines, with a minimum of 3 in each. A face-up player heads up each line about 4 yards away.
2. X3 and X6 start with a ball and simultaneously pass to the face-up players (X1 and X2). They then sprint to the back of the group.
3. The face-up pair pass back to X4 and X7 respectively, then change places quickly.
4. X1 will now receive the next ball from X7 and X2 from X4.
5. The drill continues.

GENERAL TRAINING DRILL   **PRACTICE 15**

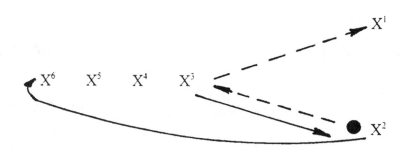

1. The players form 1 line, with 2 face-up players about 4 yards away. X2 starts with a ball.
2. X2 passes to X3 and sprints to the back of the line.
3. X3 returns to the ball first time to X1, then runs to take X2's place.
4. X1 passes back to X4 and sprints to the back of the line.
5. X4 returns the ball to X3, then runs to take X1's place.
6. The drill continues.

GENERAL TRAINING DRILL   **PRACTICE 16**

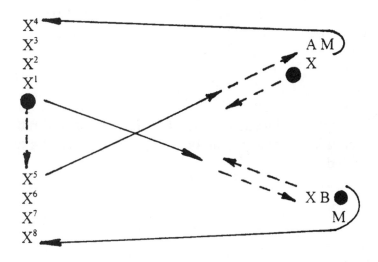

1. 4 or more players line up facing each other, in 2 rows. 1 stationary player, with a ball, at A and B. 1 ball with X1.
2. X1 passes to X5 and runs towards the player at B, who plays a 1 / 2 with him. X5 then sprints around the marker and joins the opposite file.
3. The drill continues. Replace the players at A and B regularly.

Variation
Place A and B on the other side of the lines.

NB: To increase the fitness aspect of the exercise, either place the markers further away or reduce the size of the group.

GENERAL TRAINING DRILL   PRACTICE 17

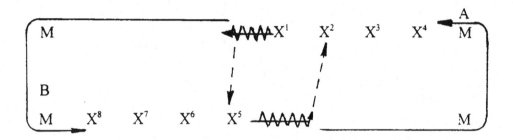

1. Set up 4 markers in a rectangle about 40 yards long and 5 yards wide. 4 or more players per group. The players of A and B stand in front of their markers. One ball with X1.
2. X1 dribbles towards group B: the first player of group B (X5), runs towards him. When they meet, X1 passes the ball into X5's running path, then sprints around the 2 markers and joins the back of the opposite group.
3. X5 dribbles towards X2, who is running towards him and passes the ball into his running path. He then sprints around the end markers and joins the back of the opposite group.
4. The drill continues.

Variations
a) Players run in a clockwise direction, so that they have to pass with their left foot.
b) The distance between the markers can be varied. The greater the distance the more running demanded.

GENERAL TRAINING DRILL   **PRACTICE 18**

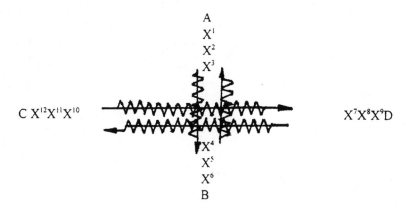

1. Line up in 4 rows, with A and B opposite each other and C and D opposite each other, as in the diagram. Players at the front of the lines have a ball each.
2. On the given signal, players dribble across the opposite line, avoiding other players in the process.
3. Encourage the players to get their heads up while dribbling and change pace.
4. The drill continues.

Variations

a) Players dribble to the middle, then pass to the opposite line and follow their pass.
b) Players dribble to the middle, pass to their RIGHT, then sprint to the end of the opposite line.
c) Players dribble to the middle, pass to their LEFT, then sprint to the end of the opposite line.
d) Players dribble to the middle, pass to their RIGHT, then follow the pass to the back of that line.

NB: The practice can be made harder by placing the lines further apart or by putting markers at the back of each line, which the incoming player must sprint around.

GENERAL TRAINING DRILL   **PRACTICE 19**

1. Groups A and B stand facing each other, about 10 yards apart, as do groups C and D. The front players of A and C start with the ball.
2. The ball is passed low to the player opposite. The passer then sprints to the back of the opposite line.
3. The drill continues.

Variations

a) After passing the ball, the player runs to the back of his own group.
b) The first player of group A passes to the front player of group B. He controls the ball with a turn, dribbles around his own group and passes back to A. A then controls the ball with a turn, dribbles around his own group and passes to the next person in group B. After the pass the players go to the back of their group. C and D do the same.
c) After passing the ball, players run across to the line opposite. Thus A passes to B, then sprints across to the back of group C, while C passes to D and sprints to the back of group A.
d) After passing the ball, players join the back of the group directly across from them. Thus A passes to B and runs to the back of group D, while C passes to D and runs to the back of group B.

NB: The practice can be made harder by placing markers at the back of each line, which must be run around.

GENERAL TRAINING DRILL   **PRACTICE 20**

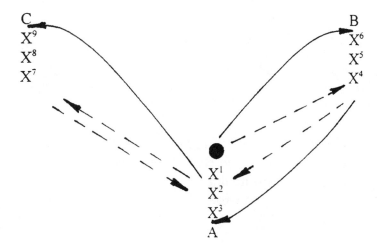

1. The players are divided into 3 lines, with no more than 3 players per line. X1 starts with the ball.
2. X1 passes to X4 and joins the back of line B. X4 returns the ball to X2 and joins the back of line A.
3. X2 passes to X7 and joins the back of line C. X7 returns the ball to X3 and joins the back of line A.
4. The drill continues.

Variations

a) After passing the ball, the player joins the back of his own group. The groups have to be moved around quite regularly.
b) X1 passes to X4 and joins the back of his own group. X4 passes to X7 and joins the back of his own group, X7 passes to X2 and joins the back of his own group. After a while, the ball should be passed in a clockwise direction.

GENERAL TRAINING DRILL   PRACTICE 21

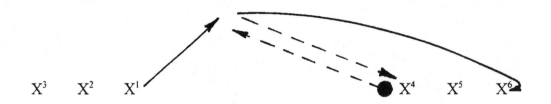

1. 3 or more players line up in 2 rows, facing each other. X4 with a ball.
2. X1 makes a run to the right or left and calls for the ball. X4 delivers it into his path and runs to the back of the opposite line.
3. X1 returns the ball to X5 and sprints to the back of that line.
4. The process starts again with X2 going to the right or the left, calling for the ball from X5 and so on.
5. The drill continues.

GENERAL TRAINING DRILL   PRACTICE 22

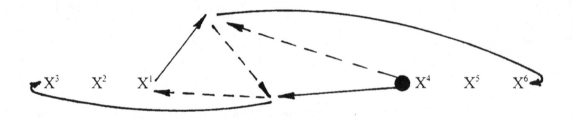

1. 3 or more players line up in 2 rows, facing each other. X4 with a ball.
2. X1 makes a run to the right or left and calls for the ball.
3. X4 delivers the ball to him, then runs out, receives a return ball and passes to X2.
4. X4 runs to the back of the opposite line, as does X1.
5. X5 now calls for the ball from X2. X2 gives it to him, gets a return ball, passes it to X6 and so on.
6. The drill continues.

GENERAL TRAINING DRILL   **PRACTICE 23**

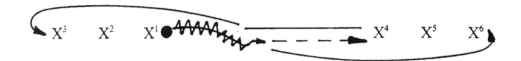

1. 3 or more players line up in 2 rows, facing each other. X1 with a ball.
2. X1 dribbles towards the opposite line of players.
3. At the same time, X4 moves towards X1 and gives passive opposition.
4. X1 feints, beats him and passes to X5.
5. Both players then sprint to the end of the opposite line.
6. X5 dribbles towards X2, who comes out to meet him and provides passive opposition and so on.
7. The drill continues.

GENERAL TRAINING DRILL   **PRACTICE 24**

1. 3 or more players line up in 2 rows, facing each other. X1 with a ball.
2. X1 passes to X4 and sprints to the back of the opposite line.
3. X4 controls the ball with one foot, passes to X2 with the other and joins the back of the opposite line.
4. Each player receiving the ball MUST take two touches - one to control and one to pass.
5. The drill continues.

GENERAL TRAINING DRILL   **PRACTICE 25**

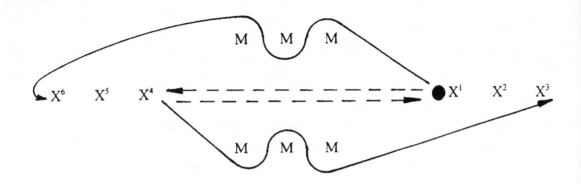

1. The players line up in 2 rows, with no more than 3 per row. 2 rows of markers are set up, with 2 yards between each. X1 starts with a ball.
2. X1 passes to X4, then runs through the markers on his right and joins the back of the opposite line.
3. X4 returns the ball first time to X2, then runs through the markers on his right and joins the back of the opposite line.
4. The drill continues.

NB: The further the markers are away from the players, the harder the drill.

Variations
a) The players pass the ball and run through the markers on their left.
b) On receiving the ball, the players must take two touches.

GENERAL TRAINING DRILL   **PRACTICE 26**

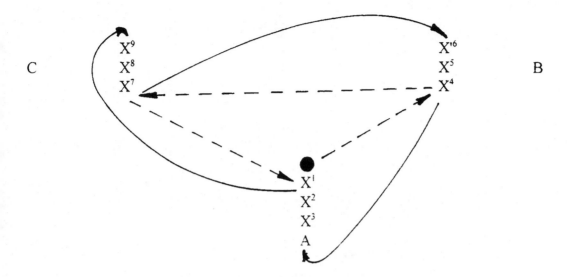

1. The players are divided into 3 rows, with no more than 3 players per row. X1 starts with the ball.
2. X1 passes to X4 and joins the back of line C.
3. X4 passes to X7 and joins the back of line A.
4. X7 plays it first time to X2 and joins the back of line B.
5. The drill continues.

Variation
After a while, the ball should be passed in a clockwise direction. This will alter the run of the players.

GENERAL TRAINING DRILL   PRACTICE 27

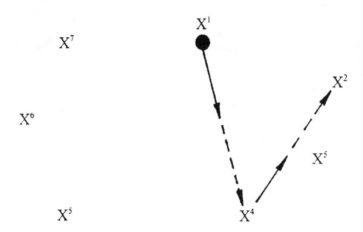

1. Any number of players form a circle.
2. X2 starts with the ball and passes to another player – in this case X4. After the pass he sprints to take the place of that player.
3. X4 then passes to X2 and follows his pass.
4. No player may pass to anybody on his immediate right or left.
5. The drill continues.

GENERAL TRAINING DRILL   PRACTICE 28

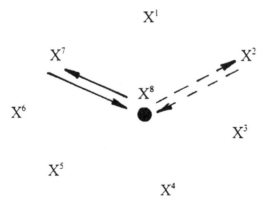

1. Any number of players form a circle, with one man in the middle (X8) with the ball.
2. X8 passes to one of the players on the outside (X2), and runs to take the place of another player (X7) who must leave his position and run to the middle of the circle.
3. The player who receives the ball (X2) lets the ball gently rebound to the center of the circle and the process starts again.
4. Encourage players to call out names when changing places.
5. The drill continues.

GENERAL TRAINING DRILL   **PRACTICE 29**

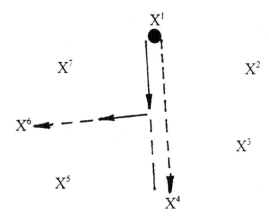

1. Any number of players form a circle.
2. X1 starts with the ball and passes to another player – in this case X4.
3. After the pass he sprints to the middle, gets a return pass from X4 and lays it off to anybody he chooses (in this case X6). He then sprints to take X6's place.
4. The drill continues.

GENERAL TRAINING DRILL   **PRACTICE 30**

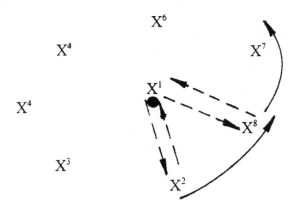

1. Any number of players form a circle, with 1 man in the middle (X1) with the ball.
2. X1 plays the ball to X2, who returns it first time, then sprints counter-clockwise around the circle and back to his place.
3. As soon as he receives the ball, X1 plays the ball to X8 who returns it first time and then sprints around the circle counter-clockwise.
4. The drill continues.
5. Change the central player frequently.

GENERAL TRAINING DRILL   **PRACTICE 31**

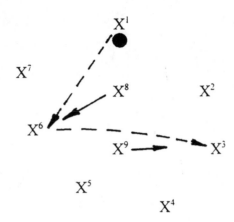

1. Any number of players form a circle, with two defenders X8 and X9 in the middle.
2. The players on the outside pass it amongst themselves and the defenders try to intercept these passes.
3. If either of them get a touch of the ball, the person on the outside who last played it changes places with one of the defenders.
4. Players on the outside are allowed 2 touches at first, but this should be reduced to 1 touch as the standard improves.

Variation
Count the number of passes and if the attackers get more than 10, then the two defenders stay in the middle, even if they intercept the ball.

GENERAL TRAINING DRILL   **PRACTICE 32**

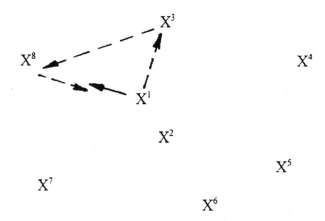

1. Any number of players form a circle, with 1 attacker and 1 defender in the middle (X1 and X2).
2. X1 starts with the ball and plays it to anybody on the outside.
3. X2 acts as a defender and attempts to intercept any passes between X1 and those in the circle.
4. The players on the outside may pass the ball amongst themselves, but then must pass to X1 if he calls for it.
5. X2 may not tackle players in the circle.
6. Work players for 2 minutes then reverse their roles.

Variations
a) If X2 wins the ball he becomes the attacker and X1 the defender.
b) As above but 2 attackers and 2 defenders in the circle.

GENERAL TRAINING DRILL   **PRACTICE 33**

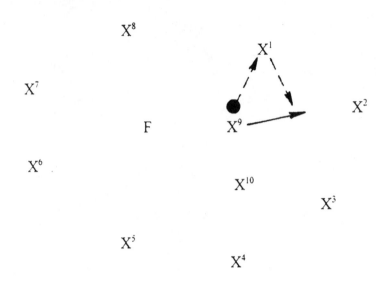

1. Any number of players form a circle, with 1 attacker and 1 defender in the middle (X9 and X10), plus 1 feeder (F).
2. The attacker (X9) starts off with the ball and plays it to anybody on the outside. He can also use the feeder, who moves around in the circle trying to make good angles.
3. The players on the outside must pass the ball first time, either amongst themselves or back to X9.
4. The defender can only steal the ball from the attacker. If he is successful, the roles are reversed.

Variation
2 versus 2 plus 1 feeder in a circle. This would be for larger groups.

GENERAL TRAINING DRILL   **PRACTICE 34**

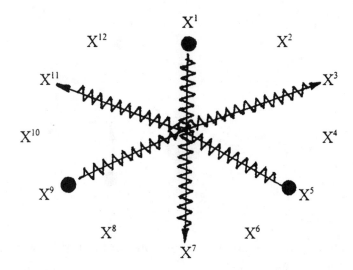

1. 12 or more players form a large circle, with 3 in possession of a ball (X1, X5, X9).
2. On a signal X1, X5, and X9 dribble across the circle, being careful to avoid each other.
3. They take the place of the person they have dribbled to and the process continues.
4. Encourage the dribblers to change pace during the run.
5. Players cannot dribble to the person to their immediate right or left.

Variations
a) Players pass the ball and follow their pass.
b) Players dribble half way, pass the ball and follow their pass.
c) Players pick up another e.g. X1 dribbles to X7 and gives him the ball. X1 turns, runs behind X7 while he dribbles across to another e.g. X3. X3 takes the ball, X7 follows him and X1 takes X3's place. The drill continues.

GENERAL TRAINING DRILL   PRACTICE 35

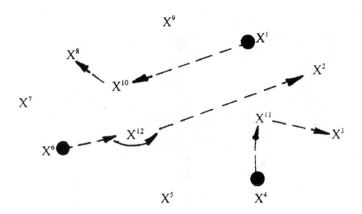

1. Any number of players form a circle, with 3 more on the inside (X10, X11, X12).
   3 players on the outside with a ball.
2. The balls are played into X10, X11 and X12 and they must pass, first time, to anybody on the outside APART from the person who gave them the ball.
3. Encourage those on the inside to look up and call.
4. Change the inside players regularly.

GENERAL TRAINING DRILL   PRACTICE 36

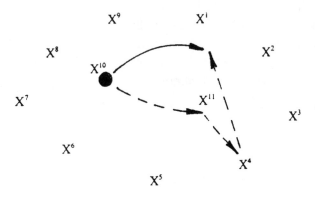

1. Any number of players form a circle, with 2 more (X10, X11) on the inside. X10 starts
   with the ball.
2. X10 passes it to X11 and moves into space.
3. X11 passes first time to anybody on the outside (in this case X4).
4. Change the inside players every two minutes.

GENERAL TRAINING DRILL   **PRACTICE 37**

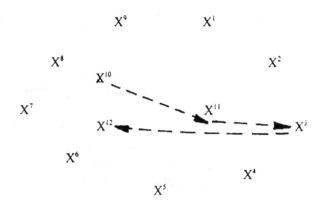

1. Any number of players form a circle with 3 players (X10, X11, X12) on the inside. X10 starts with the ball.
2. X10 passes to X11, who plays it first time to anybody on the outside. In this case X3.
3. X3 returns the ball to X12. He passes first time to X10 and the sequence starts again.
4. Change the inside players every 3 minutes.

GENERAL TRAINING DRILL   **PRACTICE 38**

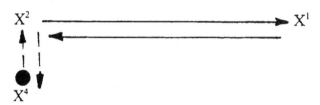

1. Players X3, X2,and X1 line up 4 yards apart. X4 faces X2 who is 5 yards away.
2. X4 has a ball and passes to X2, who immediately passes back and sprints to X1 or X3.
3. Players X1 or X3 sprint to the middle (in this case X1). He returns the pass given to him by X4 and changes places with one of the outside players.
4. The drill continues. Change the face-up player regularly.

GENERAL TRAINING DRILL   PRACTICE 39

1. 4 players line up, as in the diagram. X4 and X1 20 yards apart, with a ball each. X3 is the attacker and X2 the defender.
2. X2 calls, gets a pass from either X4 or X1 and gives it back. He might then turn sharply and get a pass from X1, or get another pass from X4.
3. X2 tries to intercept the passes. If successful, he continues as the defender.
4. This is a hard practice and after 1 minute the 2 outside players should change roles with those on the inside.
5. Every player must experience each role.

GENERAL TRAINING DRILL   PRACTICE 40

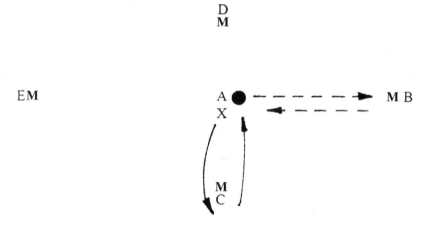

1. 5 players stand as shown in the diagram, player A with the ball.
2. Player A passes to B, and sprints to C.
3. Player C leaves his position and runs to the middle.
4. Player B passes the ball back to the middle and C passes it to D.
5. C then runs to B, who has left his position and run to the middle.
6. D returns the ball to the middle. B passes it to E and runs to take D's place.

NB: The ball must travel in the strict order above and the position changes always take place so that a player changes places with a player on his RIGHT after the pass.

Variation
Pass the ball then change places with the player on your left.

GENERAL TRAINING DRILL   **PRACTICE 41**

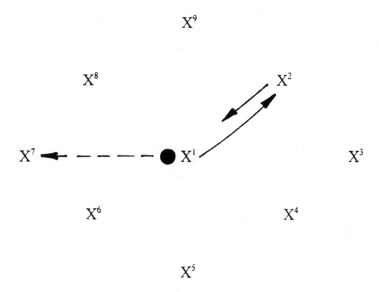

1. 6 to 10 players form a circle, with 1 in the middle with a ball.
2. X1 heads the ball to a player on the outside (X7) and immediately sprints to another (X2).
3. X2 leaves his position and sprints to the middle.
4. X7 heads the ball back to the center of the circle, where X2 catches it and the process starts again.

Variation
With experienced players, the player who has just run into the middle, instead of catching the ball, heads it directly to one player and sprints to another. The circle might need to be smaller for this drill.

GENERAL TRAINING DRILL   **PRACTICE 42**

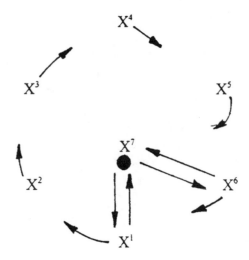

1. Any number of players form a circle, with 1 of them (X7) in the middle to act as feeder.
2. The players on the outside jog in a clockwise direction.
3. X7 passes a ball for X1 to control and pass back on the move.
4. X7 then passes to X6 and so on.
5. The middle player should always pass the ball in the opposite direction to the runners.
6. Change the middle player regularly.

Variation
a) After a time the players should run in a counter-clockwise direction.
b) Introduce a second feeder for more advanced players.
c) Use a goalkeeper as feeder, to throw the ball out.

GENERAL TRAINING DRILL   **PRACTICE 43**

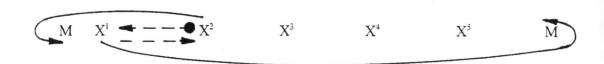

1. 4 to 6 players line up in a row, with a face-up player 5 yards away. 2 markers are set up as in the diagram. The player at the front of the line (X2) starts with the ball.
2. X2 passes to X1 and immediately sprints around the marker to X1's position.
3. X1 passes the ball back gently to X3 and sprints around the marker to the back of the line.
4. X3 passes to X2, sprints around the marker to X2's position and the drill continues.

GENERAL TRAINING DRILL   **PRACTICE 44**

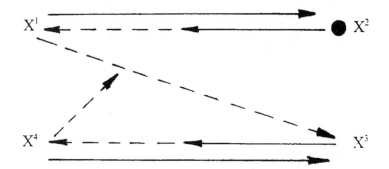

1. 4 players line up in a rectangle, with X2 starting with the ball.
2. X2 passes to X1 and follows his pass.
3. X1 passes the ball diagonally across to X3 and then changes places with X2.
4. X3 passes to X4 and follows his pass, X4 passes diagonally across to X1 and the drill continues.
5. Only the ball crosses the area.

NB: After a while the direction of passes may be changed.

GENERAL TRAINING DRILL   **PRACTICE 45**

A.

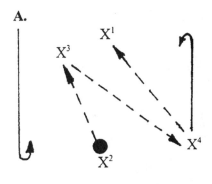

B.

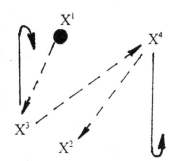

1. The players line up as in diagram A. X1 and X2, who are at least 20 yards apart, act as feeders, with X2 starting with the ball.
2. X2 passes to X3. X3 plays it first time to X4, who has made a deep angle for him.
3. X4 then plays it off to X1 and as soon as he has passed it, the two central players (X4 and X3) sprint to the line they are facing. (See diagram A.)
4. As soon as both players turn X1 feeds the ball to X3, X3 to X4, X4 to X2 and the process starts again, although both players now sprint to the opposite lines (See diagram B.)
5. Change the roles regularly as this is a strenuous exercise for the central players.

GENERAL TRAINING DRILL   **PRACTICE 46**

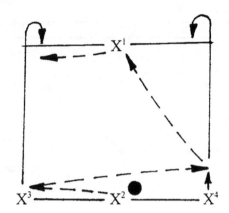

1. 4 players line up, as in the diagram. X1 and X2, who are at least 10 yards apart, act as feeders. X2 starts with the ball.
2. X2 plays a short pass to X3. X3 immediately plays a ball for X4 to run onto and he in turn gives it first time to X1.
3. Once he has played the ball, X4 sprints to the end line, turns and is ready to receive the next ball from X3 who meanwhile has sprinted to the end line in readiness for the next ball from X1.
4. Feeders and runners should change regularly, as this is a strenuous exercise for the central players.

GENERAL TRAINING DRILL

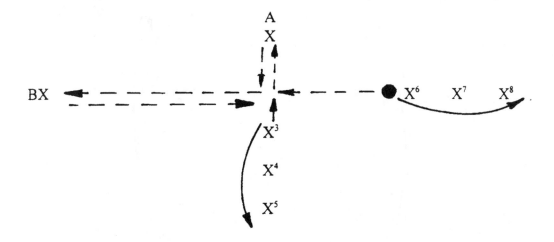

1. The players at A and B act as walls and remain in the same spot.
2. X6 starts with the ball, plays it to B and runs to the back of his line.
3. B plays the ball back first time to the middle, where X3 runs out to meet it and passes to A. X3 then runs to the back of his line.
4. A returns the ball to the middle and X7 runs out and passes to B.
5. The drill continues.

NB: To make the practice harder, markers can be placed at the back of the line, so players have further to run.

GENERAL TRAINING DRILL   PRACTICE 48

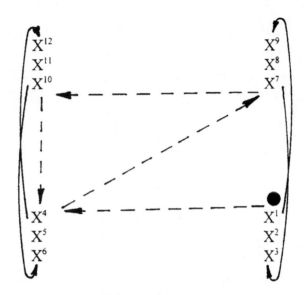

1. 4 lines are formed with a distance of 30 yards between them.
2. X1 starts with the ball and plays a short pass to X4.
3. X4 then knocks a long ball to either of the leading men in the opposite lines (in this case X7).
4. X1 and X4 then sprint to the back of the opposite lines.
5. X7 controls the ball, plays a short pass to X10 who then knocks a long ball to X2 or X5 (in this case X5).
6. X7 and X10 then sprint to the back of the opposite lines and the process starts again.

NB: The practice can be made harder by reducing the size of the group or by placing markers at the end of each line, which incoming runners have to sprint around.

GENERAL TRAINING DRILL **PRACTICE 49**

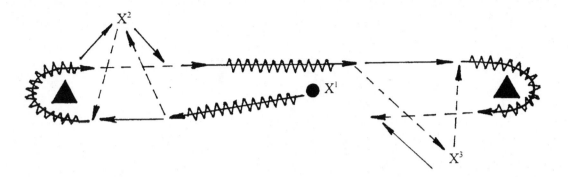

1. 2 cones are set up 40 yards apart. X2 and X3 are 10 yards from the cones.
2. X1 starts with the ball, dribbles quickly in the direction shown and plays a wall pass with X2.
3. X1 gets the return, dribbles at speed around the cone and passes the ball to X2, who has already moved in position to receive the ball. X1 then sprints to X2's position.
4. X2 dribbles the ball quickly, plays a wall pass with X3, gets the return and dribbles around the cone.
5. He delivers a pass to X3, who has already run into position to receive the ball, then sprints to take X3's place.
6. The drill continues.

Variation
The feeding players (X2 and X3) can stand across from their present positions, so that the dribbling player passes with his right foot.

GENERAL TRAINING DRILL

A   **B**

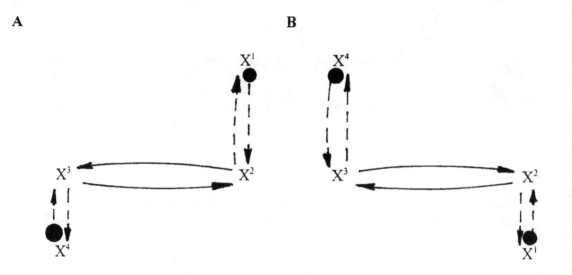

1. The players line up as in diagram A, X1 and X4 with a ball each and 5 yards from the middle players.
2. X1 plays to X2 and X4 plays to X3 simultaneously.
3. The middle players pass back first time to the outside, then turn to their left and sprint to take up each other's position.
4. X4 plays his ball to X2, X1 to X3 and the drill continues.
5. Change the middle players regularly as this can be a hard exercise.

Variation
The feeding players can stand across from their present positions (diagram B), so that the middle players must turn to their right.

GENERAL TRAINING DRILL   PRACTICE 51

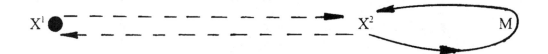

1. 2 players stand facing each other 10 yards apart.
2. X1 starts with the ball and passes to X2, who returns it first time.
3. X2 then turns and sprints around the marker.
4. At this point X1 plays the next ball in, which X2 returns first time and the drill continues.
5. Make sure X2 turns to his right and left. After 10 passes, change roles.

Variations
a) 2 touch. X2 controls the ball with 1 foot and passes with the other.
b) X1 throws the ball for X2 to head back before sprinting around the marker.
c) X1 throws the ball for X2 to volley back before sprinting around the marker.
d) X2 starts from a sitting position. He jumps up quickly, passes back to X1, sprints around the marker and sits down again, before the next ball is played in.

GENERAL TRAINING DRILL   PRACTICE 52

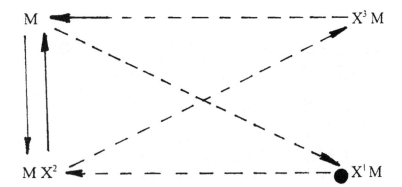

1. 4 markers are set up to form a rectangle. The distance from X1 to X2 is 15 yards and from X1 to X3, 10 yards.
2. X1 starts with the ball and passes to X2. X2 passes first time to X3 and runs to the free marker.
3. X3 passes to X2 at the free marker.
4. X2 passes first time to X1 and runs back to his starting position.
5. X1 and X3 keep their positions while X2 runs back and forth between the 2 markers.
6. Change roles regularly.

GENERAL TRAINING DRILL   PRACTICE 53

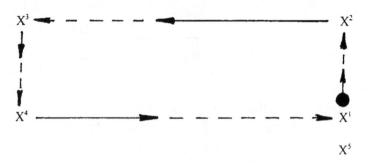

1. 5 players take up their position in a square, roughly 10 yards by 10 yards, with 2 players standing at the starting point. X1 has a ball.
2. X1 passes to X2 and follows his pass.
3. X2 passes to X3 and follows his pass and so on.
4. After a while the ball should be passed in the opposite direction.

GENERAL TRAINING DRILL   PRACTICE 54

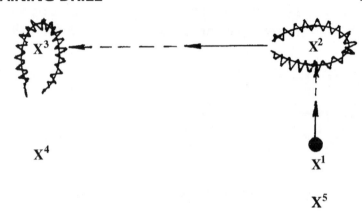

1. 5 players take up their positions in a square roughly 10 yards by 10 yards, with 2 players standing at the starting point. X1 has a ball.
2. X1 passes to X2 then runs to stop directly in front of him.
3. X2 controls the ball, dribbles around X1, passes to X3 and runs to stop directly in front of him.
4. The drill continues.
5. After a time the ball should be passed in the opposite direction.

GENERAL TRAINING DRILL   PRACTICE 55

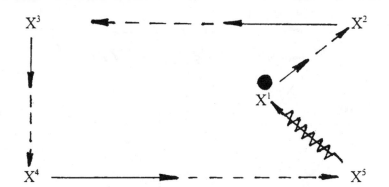

1. 5 players take up their positions in a square, roughly 10 yards by 10 yards. X1 in the middle with a ball.
2. X1 passes to X2 and follows his pass.
3. X2 passes to X3 and follows his pass and so on.
4. When the ball reaches X5, he dribbles to the middle, passes to X1 and the whole process starts again.
5. All passes should be first time.
6. After a while, go the other way around the square e.g. X1 to X5, X5 to X4 etc.

GENERAL TRAINING DRILL   PRACTICE 56

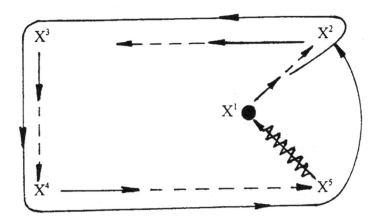

1. 5 players take up their position in a square, roughly 10 yards by 10 yards. X1 in the middle with a ball.
2. X1 passes to X2, runs around the outside of the square and takes X2's place.
3. Meanwhile X2 passes to X3 and follows his pass. X3 passes to X4 and follows his pass and so on.
4. When X5 receives the ball, he dribbles to the middle, passes to X1, runs around the outside of the square and takes X1's place.
5. The drill continues.
6. After a time go the other way around the square e.g. X1 to X5 and sprint around the outside to take X5's place etc.

GENERAL TRAINING DRILL **PRACTICE 57**

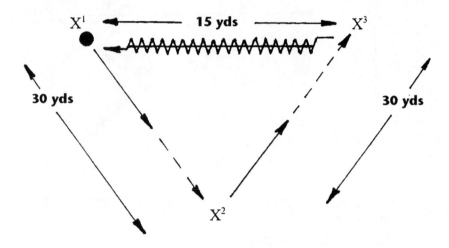

1. 3 players line up in a triangular formation. X1 starts with the ball.
2. X1 drives a low ball to X2 and sprints to his position.
3. X2 controls the ball, chips to X3 and sprints to his position.
4. X3 controls the ball, dribbles slowly to X1's position, then drives a low ball to X1 and sprints after it.
5. The drill continues.
6. After a certain time players pass and run in the opposite direction.

GENERAL TRAINING DRILL   **PRACTICE 58**

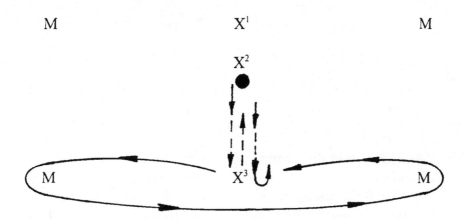

1. 3 players line up as in the diagram, at least 20 yards apart. X2 has a ball and stands just in front of X1. 2 markers are placed 7 yards to either side of the end players.
2. X2 passes to X3, gets a return ball, plays it back to X3 and sprints to collect it.
3. X3 leaves the ball at his position, sprints to the markers on his left and right, then returns to his position.
4. Meanwhile X2, who has collected the stationary ball, passes to X1, gets a return ball, plays it back to X1 and sprints to collect it.
5. X1 leaves the ball at his position, sprints to the markers on his left and right, then returns to his position.
6. The drill continues.
7. Change the central player regularly as this is a strenuous exercise.

GENERAL TRAINING DRILL

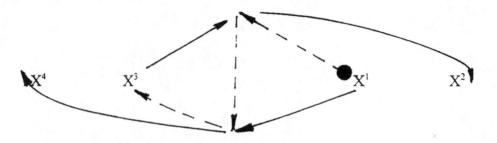

1. 4 players sit in a row about 25 yards apart.
2. X1 has a ball and throws it high, at a slight angle forward, with both hands over his head. He immediately jumps up and runs wide towards X4's position.
3. As soon as the ball is thrown, X3 jumps up, sprints towards the ball and passes it first time into X1's running path.
4. X1 passes to X4, who is still sitting and takes his place. X4 throws the ball overhead with both hands and the drill starts again.
5. This exercise is particularly good for endurance and agility if it is restricted to 4 players per group.

GENERAL TRAINING DRILL　　　　　　　　　　　　　**PRACTICE 60**

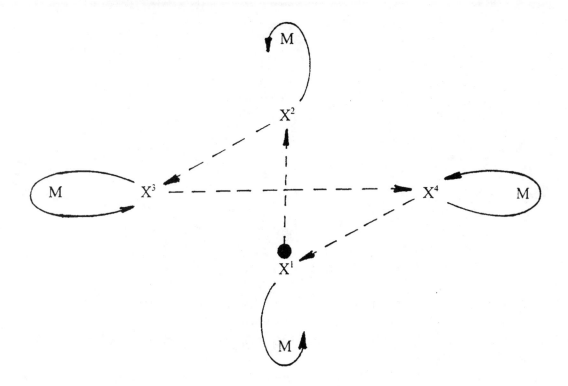

1. 4 players line up as in the diagram, each standing 5 yards from a marker. X1 starts with the ball.
2. X1 plays the ball to X2, X2 to X3, X3 to X4 and X4 back to X1.
3. After each player has passed the ball, he turns to his left and sprints around the marker behind him and back to his place.
4. Players should attempt to play the ball first time.

Variations
a) Pass the ball the opposite way around: X1 to X2, X2 to X4, X4 to X3 and back to X1.
b) Players turn to their right and sprint the other way around the markers.
c) Allow players to have a go in each position.
d) To make the practice harder place the markers further back.

GENERAL TRAINING DRILL   **PRACTICE 61**

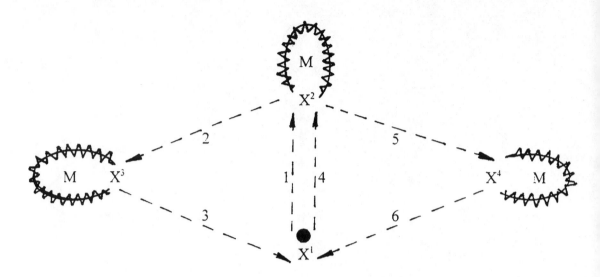

1. 4 players line up as in the diagram, 3 of them standing 10 yards in front of a marker. X1 is the feeding player and starts with the ball.
2. X1 passes to X2, who runs towards the ball, turns quickly, dribbles around the marker and passes to X3.
3. X3 runs towards the ball, turns quickly, dribbles around the marker and passes to X1.
4. X1 passes back to X2 and the process starts again on the other side.
5. Players should change positions regularly.

GENERAL TRAINING DRILL   PRACTICE 62

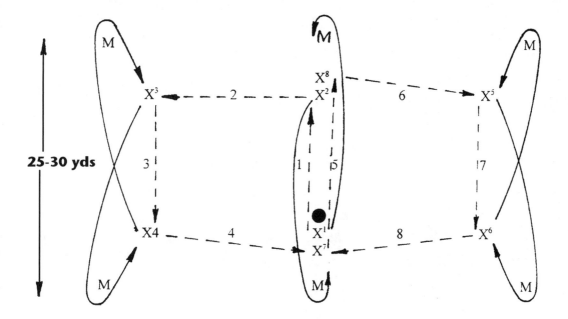

1. 8 players line up as in the diagram, with 4 players in the central row and 4 in the 2 outside rows. The markers are 25-30 yards apart in each row. The players always sprint the row they are in.
2. X1 starts with the ball, passes to X2, sprints around the marker in front of him and joins the back of that line.
3. X2 passes to X3, but sprints around the marker facing him in his row and joins the back of that line.
4. X3 passes to X4 and sprints around the marker to take X4's place.
5. X4 passes to X7, but sprints around the marker in front of him and takes X3's place.
6. The drill continues with the ball passing around the left row. (X7 to X8, X8 to X5, X5 to X6 and X6 to X7).
7. The drill can be made harder by only having 2 players in the middle row.

GENERAL TRAINING DRILL PRACTICE 63

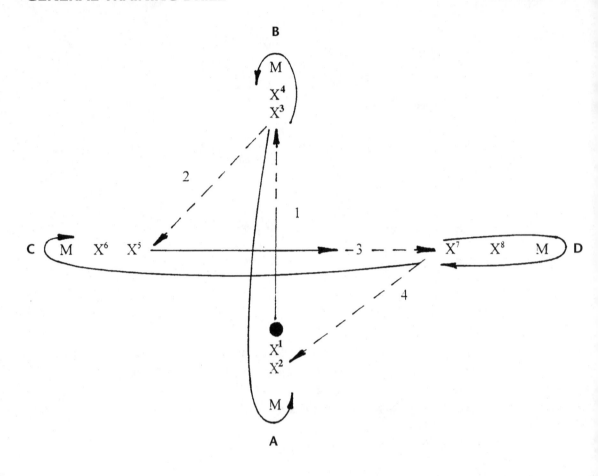

1. 8 players line up as in the diagram, with the ball passing in the order indicated. X1 starts with the ball. The markers in each row are 25-30 yards apart.
2. X1 passes to X3, sprints around the marker at B and joins the back of that line.
3. X3 passes first time to X5, but sprints around the marker at A and joins the back of that line.
4. X5 passes to X7, sprints around the marker at D and joins the back of that line.
5. X7 passes to X2, but sprints around the marker at D and joins the back of that line.
6. The drill continues. Make sure the players work in both rows.
7. After a while the ball should be passed in the opposite direction.

GENERAL TRAINING DRILL   **PRACTICE 64**

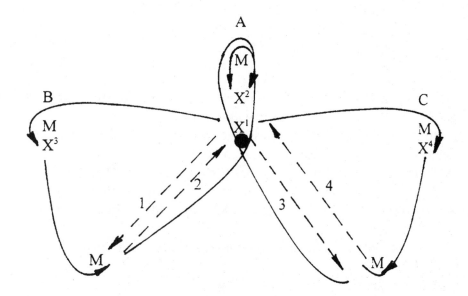

1. 4 players line up as in the diagram, with 2 at marker A and 1 each at markers B and C. X1 starts with the ball.
2. X3 sprints diagonally towards the marker in front of him and gets in position for a pass from X1.
3. X1 passes the ball at the correct moment, then sprints around the marker to take X3's place.
4. X3 immediately plays the ball back to X2, follows his pass and joins the back of the central line.
5. X4 sprints diagonally towards the marker in front of him and gets in position for a pass from X2.
6. X2 passes the ball at the correct moment, then sprints around the marker to take X4's place.
7. X4 immediately plays the ball back to X3, follows his pass and joins the back of the central line.
8. The drill continues.

GENERAL TRAINING DRILL   **PRACTICE 65**

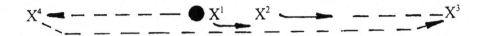

1. Players line up as in the diagram, with X4 and X3 at least 20 yards apart. X1 and X2 act as attacker and defender. X1 starts with the ball.
2. X1 passes to X4, with X2 providing passive opposition.
3. On receiving the ball, X4 passes first time to X3.
4. X1 and X2 turn sharply. X2 now becomes the attacker and X1 the defender.
5. When ready, X2 calls for the ball, holds it up, and then passes it back to X3.
6. X3 passes first time to X4. X1 and X2 turn sharply, with X1 becoming the attacker and X2 the defender.
7. The drill continues, with the defender becoming more active once the practice is understood.
8. The players must experience each role.

GENERAL TRAINING DRILL   **PRACTICE 66**

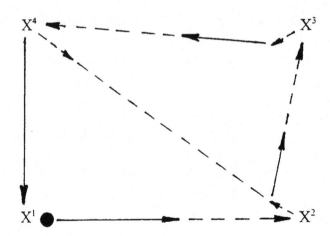

1. 4 players stand at the corners of a 10 yard square. X1 has the ball.
2. X1 passes to X2 and follows his pass.
3. X2 sets the ball up. X1 passes to X3 and follows his pass.
4. X3 sets the ball up. X1 passes to X4 and follows his pass.
5. X4 sets the ball up. X1 passes diagonally to X2 then returns to his original position.
6. The process continues with X2 passing to X3 and following his pass. X3 sets the ball up for X2 to pass to X4 and so on.

GENERAL TRAINING DRILL **PRACTICE 67**

1. 8 players line up as in the diagram with X1 and X3 having a ball each.
2. X1 passes to X5, who sets up a square ball for X1 to pass to X4.
3. Simultaneously X3 passes to X7, who sets up a square ball for X3 to pass to X2.
4. After they have passed the ball, X1 and X3 sprint to the back of the opposite line.
5. After X5 and X7 have set up the pass, they turn to their right, sprint around the marker behind them and rejoin their line.
6. The drill continues.
7. Make sure players work in both lines.

Variation
X1 passes to X7 and X3 passes to X5. This will ensure that players use their left foot on the second pass. The central players turn to their left once they have set up the pass.

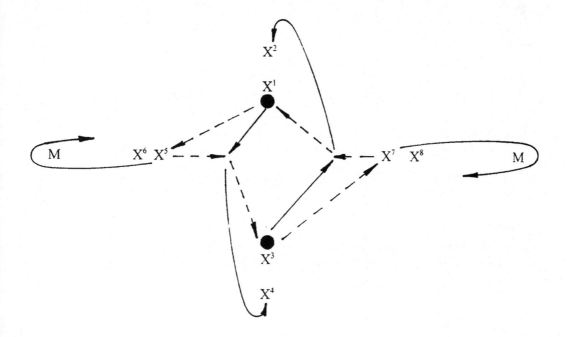

GENERAL TRAINING DRILL   **PRACTICE 68**

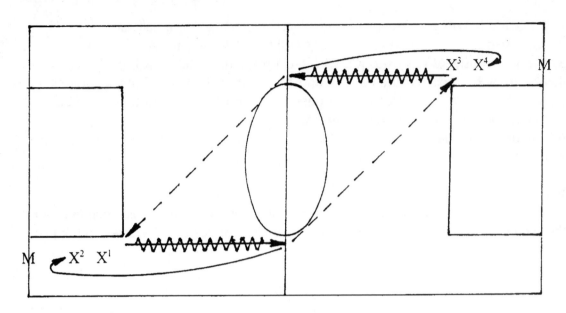

1. 4 players line up on the right corners of the 2 penalty areas.
2. X1 starts with the ball, dribbles at speed to the half-way line and plays a long pass to X3.
3. X1 turns and sprints back to his group.
4. X3 controls the ball, dribbles at speed to the half-way line and plays a long pass to X2.
5. X3 turns and sprints back to his group.
6. The drill continues.

Variations
a) To make the practice harder, 2 markers can be placed on the goal line behind each group, which have to be sprinted around on the return run.
b) Line players up on the left corners of the 2 penalty areas.

GENERAL TRAINING DRILL   **PRACTICE 69**

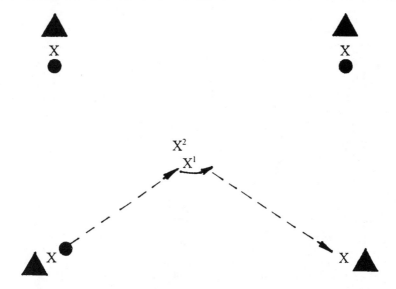

1. The players are in teams of 6, each team in a 20 x 20 yard square marked by cones.
2. A player stands in each corner, 3 of these players have a ball. The 4th player does not have a ball and acts as the first receiver. None of the corner players may move more than 2 yards in any direction from their corner.
3. The 2 players in the square are designated attacker (X1) and defender (X2). X1 can move where he likes in the square and collect a pass from any of the players with a ball.
4. On receiving the ball, X1 moves and dribbles to get away from X2 and then passes to the corner player without a ball.
5. Once successful he moves around the square, collects another pass from one of the corners and delivers it to the player without the ball.
6. The drill continues for 2 minutes, then the middle pair are replaced.
7. Make sure all players act as attacker and defender.

GENERAL TRAINING DRILL

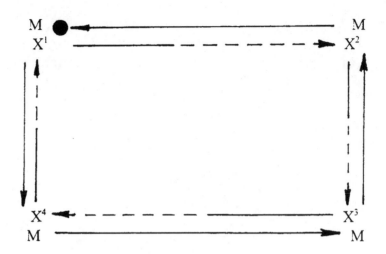

1. 4 players stand at the corners of a 10 yard square. X1 has a ball.
2. X1 passes to X2, then follows his pass, touches the marker at the receiver's corner, and returns to his original position.
3. X2 passes to X3, follows his pass, touches the marker at the receiver's corner, and returns to his original position.
4. The drill continues with X3 and X4 following the same pattern.
5. Work for a set time or set number of laps.

Variations

a) The ball is passed in a counter-clockwise direction, with the players following their pass.
b) The ball is passed in a counter-clockwise direction, but the players run in a clockwise direction.
c) Players sprint to the marker, then run backwards to their original position.
d) Players sprint to the marker, then run sideways to their original position.

GENERAL TRAINING DRILL

PRACTICE 71

A

M   X³ X¹●∿∿X² □□□□□□   X⁴   M

B

M   X³   □□□□□□ X¹◄∿∿∿●X⁴   M

X²

1. 4 players line up as in diagram A. X3 and X4 are 30 yards apart. X1 starts with a ball and X2 acts as a passive defender.
2. X1 dribbles at speed towards X2, who merely jockeys backwards.
3. X1 plays a short pass to X4 and then becomes the passive defender. See diagram B.
4. X4 now dribbles at speed towards X1, who merely jockeys backwards.
5. Meanwhile X2, once he nears the end line, turns sharply, sprints around the marker and takes up X4's position.
6. The drill continues with X3 becoming the attacking player and X4 the passive defender.
7. X4, once he nears the end line, turns sharply, sprints around the marker and takes up X3's position.

GENERAL TRAINING DRILL

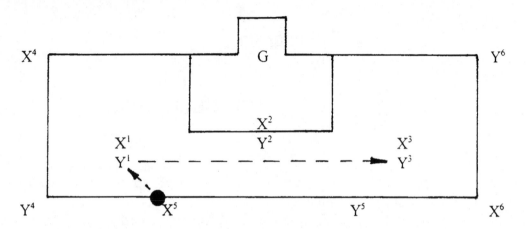

1. 13 players are required for this practice. A goalkeeper, 6 in the penalty area and 6 support players stationed around the outside. Several balls should be available.
2. The goalkeeper starts the game by throwing the ball to anybody on the outside of the penalty area.
3. The coach then says which team are in possession of the ball (in this case Y's)
4. The players on the outside are merely feeders and so have to play the ball to Y1, Y2 or Y3.
5. The Y's then try to score by playing the ball amongst themselves, or using the people on the outside, until an opening occurs.
6. If X's gain possession of the ball, then they can score and those on the outside support them.
7. If the goalkeeper gets the ball, a goal is scored or it goes out of play, then the ball is returned to anybody on the outside and the practice starts again.
8. The players on the outside cannot be tackled by the defending team.
9. After 3 minutes, those on the outside change places with those on the inside.

GENERAL TRAINING DRILL   **PRACTICE 73**

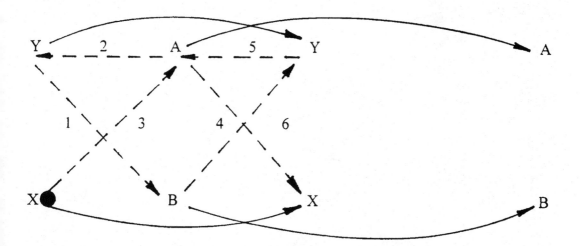

1. 4 players stand on the corners of a 10 yard square. X starts with the ball.
2. He plays a diagonal pass to A, then sprints 10 yards in front of B.
3. A passes to Y, who plays a diagonal ball to B, then sprints 10 yards in front of A.
4. The process starts again, with B playing a diagonal ball to Y, then sprinting 10 yards in front of X and Y passing to A, who plays a diagonal ball to X, then sprints 10 yards in front of Y.
5. The exercise continues the full length of the pitch and back.

GENERAL TRAINING DRILL   **PRACTICE 74**

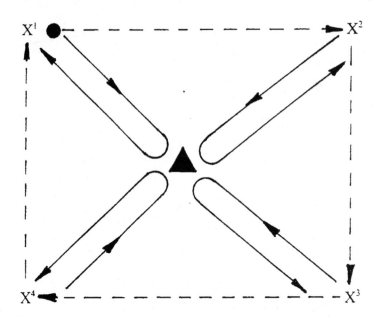

1. 4 players stand at the corners of a 15 yard square. A cone is placed in the center of the square. X1 starts with a ball.
2. X1 passes to X2, then runs forward, touches the middle cone and sprints back to his place.
3. X2 passes to X3, runs forward, touches the middle cone and sprints back to his place.
4. X3 and X4 follow the same pattern.
5. Players work for a set time e.g. 3 minutes.

Variations
a) The ball is passed in a counter-clockwise direction.
b) Players sprint to the middle cone and run backwards to their corner.
c) Players sprint to the middle cone and run sideways to their corner.
d) Players jump in the air, sit down, touch the ground with both hands etc, before sprinting to the middle.

GENERAL TRAINING DRILL   **PRACTICE 75**

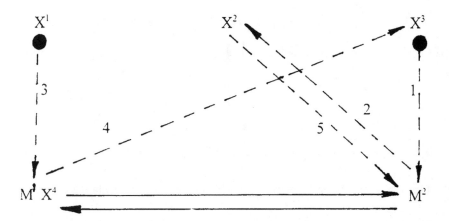

1. 4 players position themselves as in the diagram. X1 and X3 have a ball each. X4 is the free player and always passes to the free man.
2. X4 starts at M1 and shuttles to M2 and back. He can only receive the ball at M1 or M2.
3. He receives the ball from X3 and passes to X2.
4. He runs back to M1, collects a pass from X1 and passes to X3.
5. He runs back to M2, collects a pass from X2 and passes to X1.
6. The practice continues for a set time. The players then change positions.

GENERAL TRAINING DRILL   **PRACTICE 76**

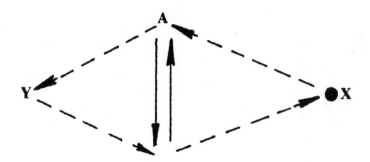

1. 3 players line up as in the diagram. X and Y are approximately 12 yards apart. X starts with the ball.
2. X passes to A, who takes the ball on his back foot and passes to Y.
3. A then runs across to the other side, receives a pass from Y, which he takes on his back foot and passes to X.
4. A moves to the other side to receive the next pass from X.
5. Work for 30 to 40 seconds, then change roles.

Variations
a) Work the ball the other way around so that A has to take the ball on his left foot.
b) A makes a curved run.
c) Shorten the distance between X and Y to 4 yards.

GENERAL TRAINING DRILL **PRACTICE 77**

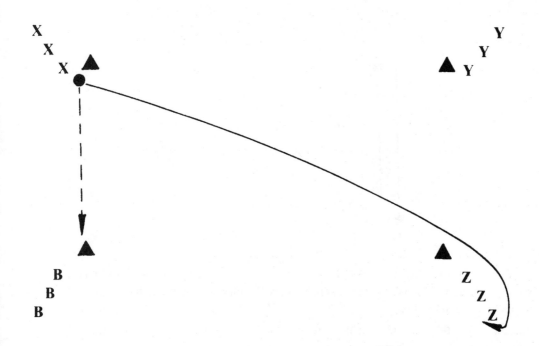

1. The players are divided into 4 lines and each line stands at a corner of a 10 yard grid. There should be no more than 3 players per line.
2. X starts with the ball and passes to any corner but CANNOT run to the corner he has passed the ball to.
3. As the number in each line changes, the player should pass the ball to the corner with the most players.
4. The coach should stipulate the number of touches.

Variation
Reduce the grid to a 4 yard square. This speeds up the passing and quickens the feet.

GENERAL TRAINING DRILL   **PRACTICE 78**

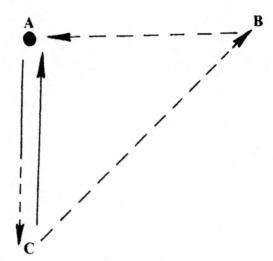

1. 3 players form a triangle. The distance form A to B and A to C is 10 yards.
2. B is the perpendicular player and remains stationary. A starts with a ball.
3. A passes to C and follows his pass.
4. C passes first time to B, but runs to A's starting position.
5. B passes first time to C's new position.
6. C passes to A, follows his pass and the process starts again.
7. Change B after a set time e.g. 1 minute.

Variations
a) Place B on the opposite side.
b) Two touch.
c) Receive with the outside of the foot, pass with the instep.
d) Receive with the inside of the foot, pass with the outside.

SUMMARY

1. The aim of this section is to provide soccer-related drills which will improve a player's technique in passing, heading, ball control and dribbling and at the same time improve soccer fitness.
2. The technical element required in these practices is too complex for players under 10 years of age. Since children of this age have little idea of time and space, they should concentrate instead on perfecting individual technique. It is only when the social skills develop, around the age of 11, that the emphasis should be on working groups.
3. Since physical conditioning does not have a major role to play for those between 10 and 14 years of age, the practices must be adapted by either shortening the distances shown or increasing the size of the groups.
4. The principles of exercise physiology must be understood by the coach when using these drills.
5. If conditioning for starting strength is required then the concentration, after passing the ball, should be on the strength of the first 3 steps.
6. If conditioning for acceleration is required, the concentration after passing the ball should be on a faster stride rate.
7. If the emphasis is on speed, then the drills should be performed near the start of the session with the size of the groups numbering at least 6 and the distance sprinted no more than 20 yards.
8. If the coach wishes to condition endurance, then the size of the group should be reduced, the distances increased and the practice continuous for between 3 to 6 minutes.
9. If conditioning for speed endurance is required, then the aim should be to maintain top speed for as long as possible. To ensure that this is achieved, the group should remain small, the files placed further apart and the players encouraged to work maximally for between 35 to 50 seconds.
10. These drills are designed to be as close to a game situation as possible and if the coach sets up the exercise correctly, players should be able to improve fitness levels and practice their skills at the same time.

SPEED AND AGILITY

Sir Stanley Matthews always said that the secret of soccer was not pace, but a change of pace. He used to practice 20 sprints a day over 15 yards. It is interesting to note that the mean duration of a sprint during Danish top class matches, according to Bangsbo, is only 2 seconds or about 17 yards. Therefore the person who is fastest over the first 20 yards of a 100 yard race, but comes in last, has the type of speed suitable for soccer.

What form should speed training take? It is very easy for a coach to organize formal speed training, where players sprint in a straight line over a certain distance. This, however, has little relevance to soccer, since it does not involve anticipation, reaction to stimuli or changes of direction. It is essential that time be spent instead on functional speed training, which might involve a ball and reaction to it or a variety of exercises which demand changes in speed, direction, body gravity and the frequency and length of the stride.

Soccer is a game of 2 to 20 yard bursts and so a soccer player rarely reaches top speed. Acceleration is therefore the most important part of running in soccer and is largely determined by the strength of the first step. This step requires the greatest muscle power, the second a little less and so on up to the fifth step. At this point, the player should be up to speed. The coach should forget about training players to be 100 yard sprinters and should concentrate instead on developing explosion in the first 5 steps.

In training it is necessary to distinguish between stationary starts and starts with a forward motion. In the former, the player must have enough strength to overcome gravity and if he is weak on his first step, then extra power training is necessary. This can be achieved through weight training, resistance training, plyometrics and body weight movements, but once again it must be soccer specific strength, so much of the resistance work has to be done in short, explosive motions.

Stationary starts need to be integrated within the framework of soccer related actions. To do this, 2 or more activities can be joined together and this combining is referred to as 'coupling.' The sort of actions needed to bring this about are:

1. Stand square to a line + sprinting (Ensure players don't take one step back before sprinting)
2. Stand sideways to a line + sprinting.
3. Stand with back to a line + sprinting.
4. Kneel on one knee + sprinting.
5. Kneel on both knees + sprinting.
6. Crouch + sprinting.
7. Lie on front + sprinting.
8. Lie on back + sprinting.
9. Lie on front, roll over + sprinting.

The sprint should be no more than 15 yards and could be in a straight line or an arc. The sprint could end with a pass, tackle, shot or header.

With a flying start, top speed can be achieved more quickly because the first steps require less strength and energy. Like stationary starts, flying starts must be incorporated within the framework of soccer related actions. Thus co-ordination exercises can be coupled with an explosive short sprint. The sort of actions needed to bring this about are:

1. Walk 3 steps to a line + sprinting.
2. Jog 3 steps to a line + sprinting.
3. Walk backwards to a line + sprinting.
4. Jog backwards to a line + sprinting.
5. Hop 3 steps + sprinting.
6. Hop backwards one step + sprinting.
7. Hop sideways one step + sprinting.
8. Jump backwards and forwards + sprinting.
9. Run, jump to head a ball + sprinting.
10. Run backwards, jump to head a ball + sprinting.
11. Jump, turn 180° + sprinting.
12. Shuffle sideways + sprinting.
13. Jump forwards over a cone + sprinting.
14. Jump backwards over a cone + sprinting.
15. Jump sideways over a cone + sprinting.
16. Hop over a cone + sprinting.
17. Run, turn 360° + sprinting.
18. Run, jump, turn 360° + sprinting.

Jumping, landing, spinning, turning and orientation must be practiced and by integrating them with a sprint, a soccer specific action can be achieved. The number of coupling drills is endless – the only restriction is the imagination of the coach.

Learning to lean correctly at the start of a sprint is also vital for soccer players. As the player builds up speed the body should be in a deep lean, in order to overcome gravity. It should be possible to draw a straight line from the ankle of the supporting leg, through the knee, hip, torso, shoulder and ear.

To practice this position, players work in pairs. The working player leans into his partner, who extends his hands and holds his shoulders. The working player leans 45° and drives forward while his partner backpedals for 10 yards. The support player then turns to one side and lets go and the working player sprints for 15 yards.

The coach must understand that you cannot do just soccer training and hope to improve speed, balance, acceleration, and agility. Although playing games will help aerobic endurance, anticipation and decision making and improve the ability to read situations, to make the body faster and stronger requires the player to be pushed 100 per cent. The player's limits must be extended all the time and by confining training to games with a ball, these limits will not be reached and therefore speed will not be improved.

The coach must also appreciate that "you cannot run fast by training slow." By forcing the body to move faster the muscles and nerves learn to react faster. All speed training should therefore be done at the start of the session, immediately after the warm up. The work must be carried out maximally because, if not, the so-called speed program simply becomes one of speed endurance and not speed.

As previously stated, the coach needs to show creativity in his training methods and be able to analyze the type of speed movements required by players in different positions. For example, a defender might need to sprint for the return. This all involves sprinting with precise timing. The overall benefits of this type of training are far greater than those of formal training but it may not look so organized or pleasing to the eye.

I have included 65 functional speed and agility drills that will help maximize the player's speed potential, if used in the correct way. By doing these short, soccer-specific exercises, any player can learn to become more explosive around the pitch. In games success often comes down to 'a moment of truth', a point in the contest when the attacking player outmaneuvers the defense or the defense stops an attacking move. In most cases, these moments are decided by the player's speed and his ability to apply that speed in crucial game situations.

SPEED AND AGILITY   PRACTICE 1

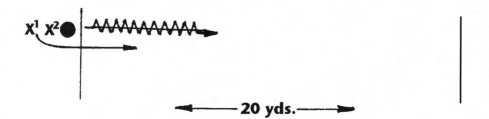

1. 2 players line up back to back, with shoulders touching. X2 has a ball.
2. As soon as X2 dribbles for the opposite line, X1 turns, chases him and attempts to reach it first.
3. Reverse roles on the way back.

SPEED AND AGILITY   PRACTICE 2

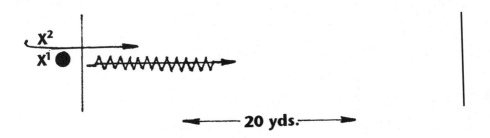

1. Players work in pairs and line up side by side but facing in opposite directions. X1 has a ball.
2. As soon as X1 touches the ball and dribbles for the line, X2 turns, chases him and attempts to reach the line first.
3. Reverse roles on the way back.

SPEED AND AGILITY   PRACTICE 3

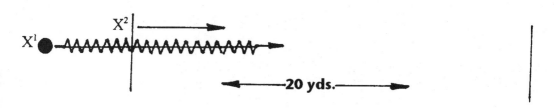

1. X1 has a ball and lines up approximately 3 yards behind X2. X2 faces the sprint line and looks ahead at all times.
2. X1 dribbles at speed, past X2. As soon as X2 spots him, he gives chase and attempts to get to the line first.
3. Reverse roles on the way back.

SPEED AND AGILITY

PRACTICE 4

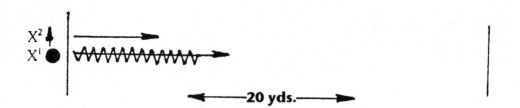

1. Players work in pairs and line up side by side. X1 has a ball.
2. As soon as X1 touches the ball and dribbles for the line, X2 jumps in the air, lands and chases him, attempting to reach the line first.
3. Reverse roles on the way back.

SPEED AND AGILITY

PRACTICE 5

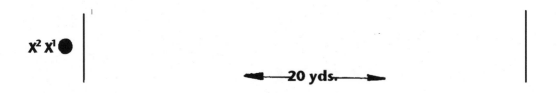

1. Players work in pairs. X1 has a ball, stands sideways, with arm up, touching X2.
2. As soon as X1 touches the ball and dribbles for the line, X2 chases attempting to reach the line first.
3. Reverse roles on the way back.

SPEED AND AGILITY   **PRACTICE 6**

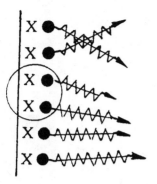 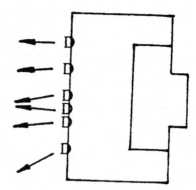

1. 4 – 8 attacking players have a ball each and line up on the half-way line.
2. A corresponding number of defenders line up facing them, on the edge of the penalty area.
3. On a signal from the coach, the attacking players have 12 seconds to dribble the ball into the penalty area and score in the empty net. They cannot shoot before reaching the penalty area.
4. The defenders try to dispossess them before they reach the penalty area. If they fail, then they attempt to stop them from shooting.
5. If an attacker loses his ball, he can then help his team mates.
6. The attackers have 3 attempts and the coach counts the number of goals scored.
7. Players then change roles.

SPEED AND AGILITY   **PRACTICE 7**

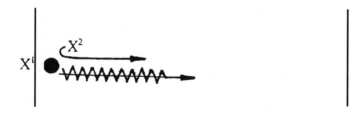

1. Players work in pairs. X1 has a ball and X2 sits down, facing him, a yard away.
2. As soon as X1 touches the ball and dribbles for the line, X2 jumps up, turns and chases him, attempting to reach the line first.
3. Reverse roles on the way back.

SPEED AND AGILITY   **PRACTICE 8**

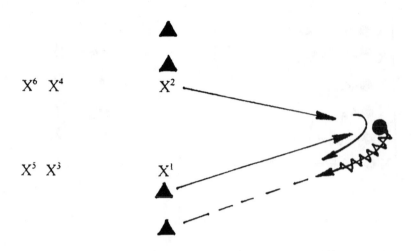

X^6 X^4 X^2

X^5 X^3 X^1

1. 2 small goals are set up about 12 yards apart. A stationary ball is placed 15 yards away. 2 players sit down next to their goals.
2. On a signal from the coach, the players jump up, sprint to the ball and attempt to dribble it back and score through their goal.
3. Players should be given a maximum of 20 seconds to achieve this. If neither score, then the next pair take their place.
4. Players can start from a variety of positions, in order to improve agility as well as speed.

SPEED AND AGILITY

PRACTICE 9

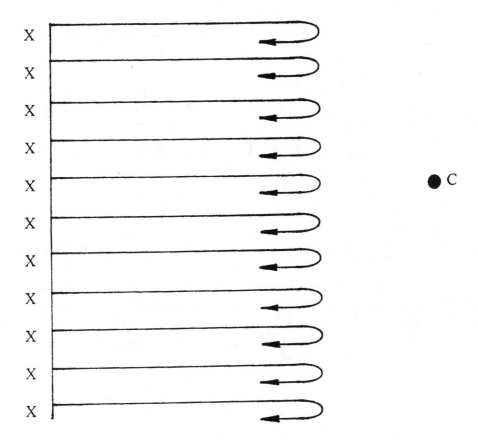

1. Players line up on the touch line facing the coach, who is about 25 yards away.
2. On a given signal, the players jog towards the coach, who is holding a ball.
3. When he bounces the ball, the players must turn and sprint for the line.
4. Make sure players turn both ways.

Variations
a) Other soccer movements such as jumping to head a ball, sitting down or touching the ground with one hand can be added before the players turn and sprint.
b) The coach either bounces the ball or throws it in the air. If he does the latter, then the players must sprint past him.

SPEED AND AGILITY   **PRACTICE 10**

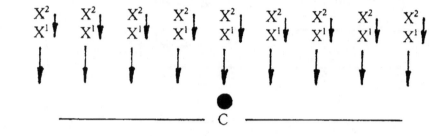

1. Players line up in pairs about 20 yards from the coach and 20 yards from the touch line, which is behind them.
2. All the X1s stand sideways, with one arm up and touching their partners.
3. The coach holds a ball and if he bounces it, the players try to beat their partners to the line on which the coach is standing.
4. If the coach throws the ball in the air, the players must turn and try to beat their partners to the touch line behind them.
5. Players change roles regularly.

SPEED AND AGILITY   **PRACTICE 11**

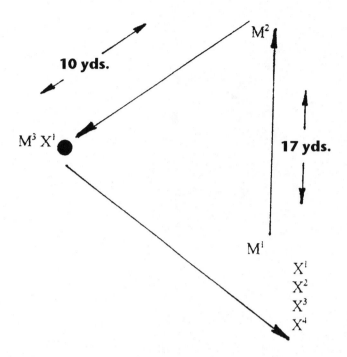

1. Players work in groups of 4 and line up as in the diagram.
2. X1 sprints from marker 1 and takes the course shown, until he reaches marker 3. Here he knocks a ball between his feet.
3. As soon as he touches the ball, X2 starts and follows the same course until he reaches X1, where he takes over the ball.
4. X1 sprints to the back of the line, X2 knocks the ball between his feet and X3 starts.
5. The course involves players changing direction and reacting to a ball.

SPEED AND AGILITY **PRACTICE 12**

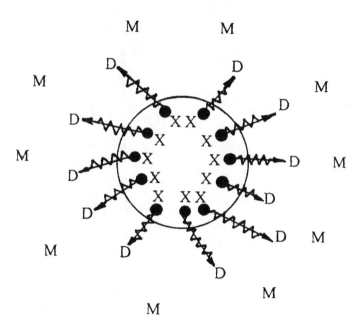

1. The players are divided into 2 teams. The attacking team starts inside the center circle and have a ball each.
2. A second circle, made with markers, is placed about 30 yards from the inner circle. All the defenders must be inside the perimeter of the outer circle.
3. On a signal from the coach, the attacking team are given a limited time (e.g. 15 sec) to dribble the ball to the edge of the outer circle.
4. The players of the defending team try to prevent this.
5. The teams alternate between attacking and defending.
6. A point is scored by players on the attacking team who reach the edge of the outer circle.

SPEED AND AGILITY   PRACTICE 13

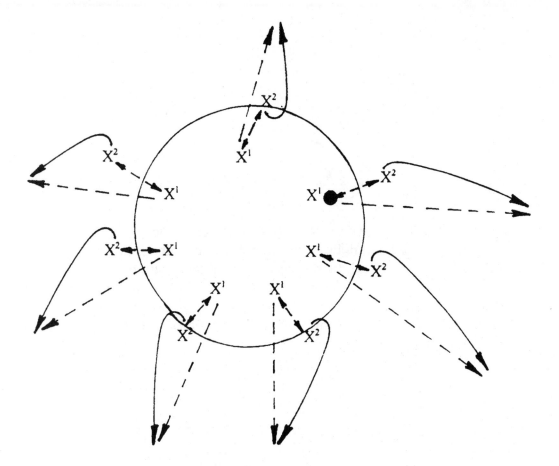

1. Players line up in pairs on the edge of the center circle, about 2 yards apart.
2. The player on the inside of the circle has a ball and passes it backwards and forwards to his partner.
3. After several passes, the inside player knocks a 20 yard ball behind his partner, who must turn and chase it.
4. On reaching the ball, X2 turns, dribbles slowly back and the practice starts again.
5. After 6 sprints, the players change roles.

NB: If it's a large group, the touch line could be used.

SPEED AND AGILITY   **PRACTICE 14**

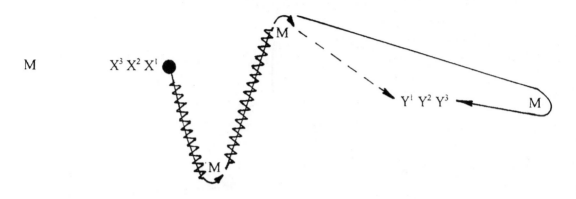

1. Players line up in 2 rows, with at least 3 players in each line.
2. X1 starts with the ball and dribbles to the first marker with his right foot.
3. He quickly changes feet and dribbles to the next marker with his left foot.
4. Once around the second marker, he passes to Y1, sprints around the marker facing him and joins the back of the line.
5. The process continues with Y1 dribbling to the first marker with his right foot, the second with his left and so on.

SPEED AND AGILITY   **PRACTICE 15**

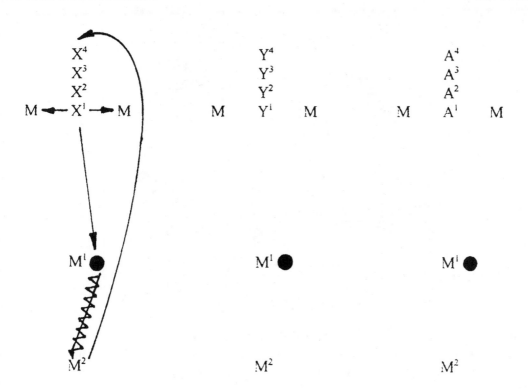

1. Players line up in rows with a minimum of 3 per line. X1, Y1 and A1 start in the middle of 2 markers, which are 3 yards apart. In front of each line are 2 more markers, with a ball at M1.
2. On a signal from the coach, the first player in the line touches the marker on his right, left, then sprints to M1, dribbles to M2, leaves the ball and sprints to the end of the line.
3. The second man in the line does not start until the coach gives the order. He follows the same pattern, but dribbles the ball back to M1.

Variations
a) Players touch the markers on their left first.
b) Players start facing the other way.
c) Players sit down, get up and then touch the markers.
d) Players jump in the air, then touch the marker.

SPEED AND AGILITY

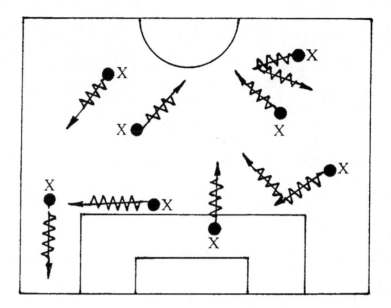

1. All the players have a ball each and work on half a soccer field.
2. They dribble slowly, then change pace and sprint with a ball for 15-20 yards.
3. They then stop the ball and move off slowly in another direction, before repeating the action.

Variations
a) Combine 2 sprints. After the first sprint, the ball is stopped dead, then dribbled at speed in another direction.
b) Without stopping the ball, the players change direction at speed, in the middle of the sprint.

SPEED AND AGILITY   **PRACTICE 17**

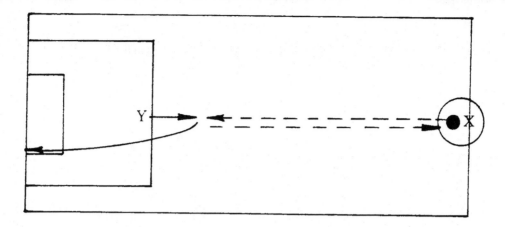

1. 2 players line up facing each other, X on the half-way line with a ball and Y on the edge of the penalty area.
2. X plays the ball firmly to Y, who sprints towards it, controls it and passes back to the feeder.
3. He then turns quickly and sprints to the goal line.
4. Players change roles after 6 sprints.

Variations
a) The type of pass from the feeder can vary e.g. low drives or chips.
b) After passing the ball back to the feeder, Y sprints to the half-way line. This practice might be more relevant for defenders.

SPEED AND AGILITY   **PRACTICE 18**

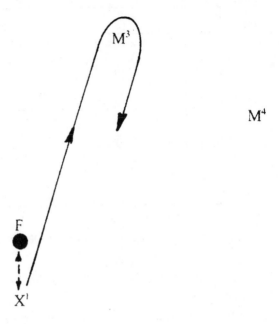

M^2

M^1

M^3

M^4

F

X^1

1. 4 different colored markers are laid down in a semi-circle. If colored markers are not available, then give each a number.
2. A feeder has a ball and plays it backwards and forwards to X1.
3. After 4 or 5 passes, the feeder stops the ball and shouts out a color or number.
4. X1 sprints around the marker called out and back to the starting point, where the process starts again.
5. After several goes, the players change roles.

Variation
To make it harder, the feeder and attacker change positions, so that the latter has his back to the markers.

SPEED AND AGILITY   PRACTICE 19

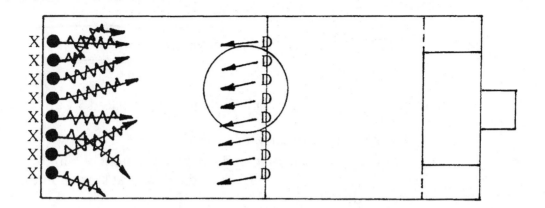

1. The players are divided into 2 teams. The attacking team starts on the goal line and have one ball each. The defending team starts on the half-way line.
2. An extended line is laid down from the corners of the opposite penalty area.
3. On a signal from the coach, the attackers attempt to dribble the length of the field and stop the ball in the extended penalty area.
4. As soon as the attackers start dribbling, the defender becomes live.
5. A point is scored by every attacker who successfully reaches the opposite penalty area.
6. The teams alternate between attacking and defending. Limit the attacking time to a maximum of 30 seconds.

SPEED AND AGILITY   PRACTICE 20

1. Players work in pairs. X1 has a ball and is 20 yards from his partner.
2. X1 dribbles at speed towards X2.
3. When X1 reaches him, X2 jockeys backwards, while X1 checks from side to side. X2 does not attempt to tackle X1.
4. On a signal from the coach, X1 turns and sprints back to where he started.
5. He passes to X2 and the roles are reversed.

Variations
a) On reaching his partner, X1 turns sideways with arm up and holds off X2. X2 provides a physical challenge but does not attempt to win the ball. On a signal from the coach, X1 sprints back to his starting point.
b) X1 dribbles at speed to his partner and plays little one-two's with him. After 4 or 5 passes, X2 plays the ball behind X1, who turns and chases after it.

SPEED AND AGILITY   PRACTICE 21

M   X² X¹ ●——————→ – – – – –→ X³   M

1. Players work in 3's and line up 20 yards apart. Two markers are placed 5 yards behind X2 and X3.
2. X1 has a ball, passes to X3 and sprints after it.
3. On reaching X3, he slows down and jogs around the marker in front of him.
4. He collects the ball from X3, passes to X2 and repeats the process at the opposite end.
5. After 6 sprints, the players change roles.

SPEED AND AGILITY   PRACTICE 22

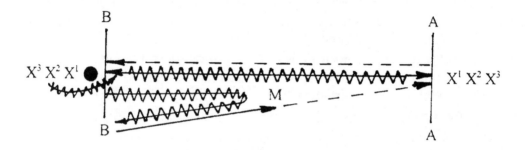

1. 3 players line up as in the diagram, 25 yards from line A. X1 has a ball.
2. X1 sprints to line A with the ball, stops and passes it back to X2.
3. X2 sprints to line A with the ball, stops and passes it back to X3.
4. X3 dribbles slowly to the marker in the middle, turns, dribbles at speed to the line his has just come from, turns again, passes to X1 and sprints to the back of the group.
5. The process starts again. Change X1 after 4 sprints.

SPEED AND AGILITY   **PRACTICE 23**

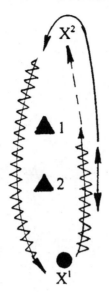

1. Players work in pairs. X1 has a ball and X2 acts as feeder. 2 cones are placed in line, 10 yards apart and 10 yards from each player.
2. X1 dribbles slowly to marker 1, where he leaves the ball.
3. He turns, sprints to marker 2 and back, collects the ball and passes to X2.
4. He sprints around X2, collects the ball and dribbles at speed back to his starting position.

SPEED AND AGILITY   PRACTICE 24

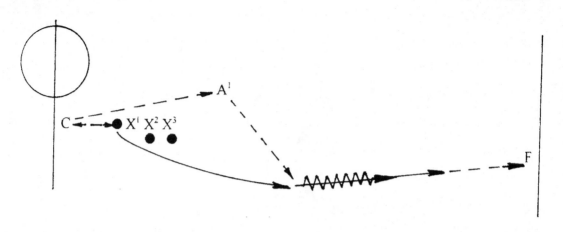

1. Players line up as in the diagram. X1, X2 and X3 have a ball each.
2. X1 plays the ball backwards and forwards with the coach. After a few passes, the coach plays the ball to A1.
3. X1 reacts to this, turns sharply to his left and gets a return ball from A1. He dribbles several paces, passes to a second feeder and sprints to collect the ball. He then rejoins the back of the line.
4. The practice continues, with the coach exchanging passes with X2.

Variations
a) A1 stands on the left hand side, so the X's have to peel off to their right.
b) The second feeder is replaced by a goal. At the end of the dribble, the X's shoot.
c) A second support player is added, so the coach can pass to either A1 or A2. The X's must react accordingly.

SPEED AND AGILITY   **PRACTICE 25**

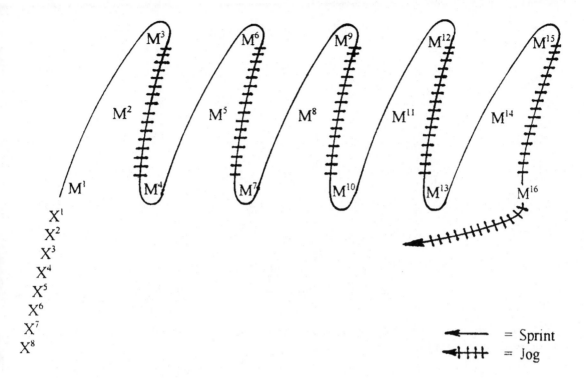

1. Players line up in one line and follow the route indicated in the diagram.
2. All players sprint to diagonals and jog the straight lines. Thus X1 will sprint from M1 to M3, sprint from M4 to M6 and so on.
3. When the first runner reaches M2, the second runner starts.

Variations
a) During the sprint, players touch the middle markers (e.g. M2) with their right hand.
b) Players touch the middle markers with their left hand.
c) Jump to head a ball before each sprint.
d) A tuck jump before each sprint.
e) Start facing the other way, before each sprint.
f) Run backwards to the middle marker, then turn and sprint for the end.

SPEED AND AGILITY   **PRACTICE 26**

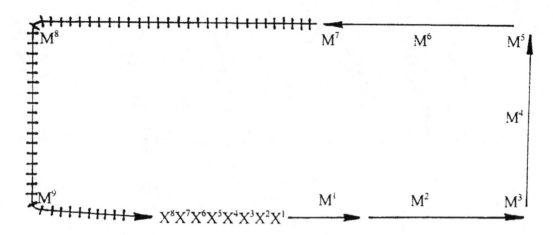

1. 6 large markers are arranged in 2 squares, 15 yards x 15 yards.
2. The runners line up in one line and start on M1. X1 sprints 3 sides of a square (M1 to M7), then jogs 3 sides of the other square and joins the back of the line.
3. X2 starts when X1 reaches the small marker (M2) in front of him.
4. The whole process is continuous.

Variations
a) Players start on M7 and sprint the other way around.
b) Jump to head a ball before sprinting.
c) Touch the 3 middle markers (M2, M4, M6) with the left hand.
d) Run backwards between markers 3 and 5.
e) Sprint to M3, stop, sprint to marker 5, stop, sprint to M7, and stop.
f) Patter (very quick feet) to marker 2, then sprint the rest of the way.

SPEED AND AGILITY   **PRACTICE 27**

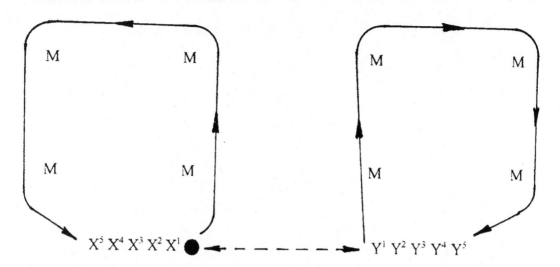

1. Players form two lines and face each other. X1 has a ball. A minimum of 4 players are required per line.
2. X1 passes to Y1, sprints around the markers on his left and joins the back of his line.
3. Y1 returns the ball first time, sprints around the markers on his right and joins the back of his line.
4. After a certain time, players change sides so that they are sprinting a different way.

SPEED AND AGILITY   PRACTICE 28

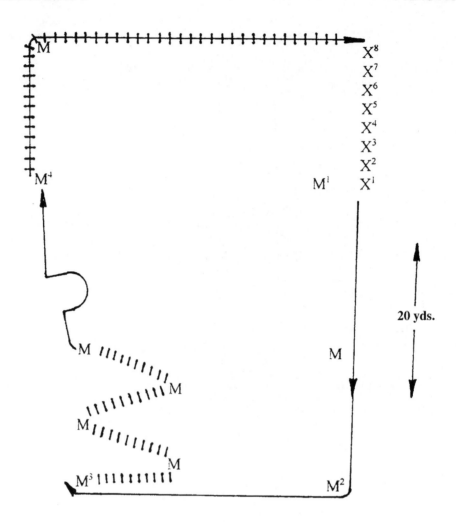

1. Players line up in one row and start at M1.
2. X1 sprints from M1 to M3 via M2. He shuffles sideways between the next 4 markers, which are 2 yards apart, jumps to head a ball and sprints to M4.
3. He jogs the next section and joins the back of the line.
4. When X1 reaches the marker between M1 and M2, X2 starts and so on.
5. Make sure runners lead with right and left leg when they shuffle sideways.
6. The whole process is continuous.

SPEED AND AGILITY   **PRACTICE 29**

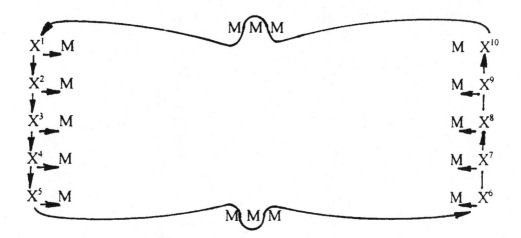

1. 10 markers are placed on the ground, 3 yards apart. 3 more are placed close
   together at either end.
2. One runner starts on each marker and follows the course shown in the diagram above.
3. All runners start simultaneously and run counter-clockwise around the square,
   touching each marker with their left hand, including the marker they started on.
4. They run in and out of the end markers.

Variations
a) As above but touch the markers with the right hand.
b) As above but touch the markers with alternate hands.
c) As above but runners travel clockwise.

SPEED AND AGILITY

PRACTICE 30

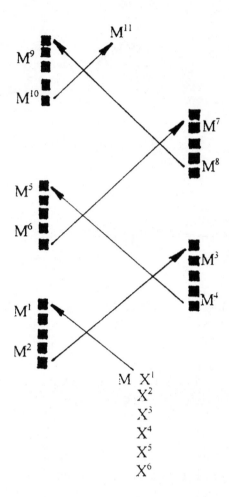

1. 5 sets of markers are placed on the ground, with each set 4 yards apart.
2. The players line up in one row.
3. X1 starts and sprints to M1. He runs backwards to M2, sprints to M3, runs backwards to M4, sprints to M5, runs backwards to M6 and so on.
4. He waits at marker 11 for everybody to finish, then the process starts again.
5. X2 starts when X1 has reached M3.

Variations
a) Runners sprint to the first marker, then jockey backwards to the second.
b) Runners touch the markers on their left with the left hand and on the right with the right hand.

SPEED AND AGILITY   **PRACTICE 31**

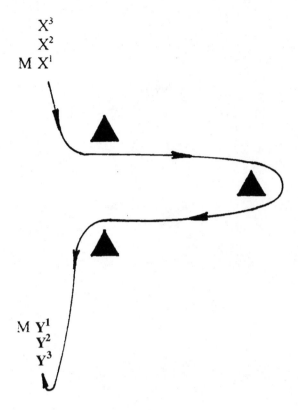

1. The runners line up in 2 rows, 20 yards apart.
2. X1 starts, sprints the course shown in the diagram and joins the back of the opposite line.
3. Y1 starts when X1 reaches him. He sprints the course the other way and joins the back of the opposite line.
4. It is a continuous relay and should last for a set time.

Variations
a) Jump to head a ball before sprinting.
b) Sit down and get up again before sprinting.
c) Run backwards to the first cone before sprinting the rest of the course.
d) Touch the ground with both hands before sprinting.

SPEED AND AGILITY

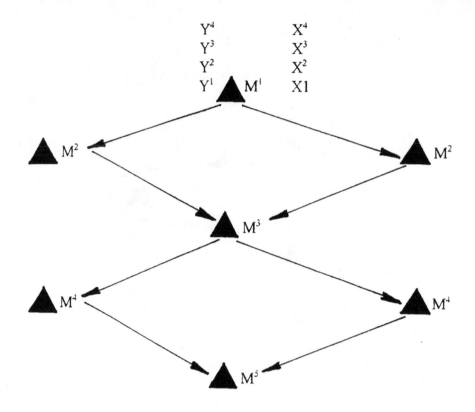

1. Players line up as in the diagram. The cones are 10 yards apart.
2. X1 and Y1 stand touching M1. On a signal from the coach, they sprint the course shown.
3. On the way they touch each cone.
4. The aim is to touch the end cone first.

Variations
a) Players run outside the wide cones.
b) Two more rows line up on cone 5. It then becomes a continuous relay.
c) Players run backwards to cone 2, then sprint the rest of the course.

SPEED AND AGILITY   **PRACTICE 33**

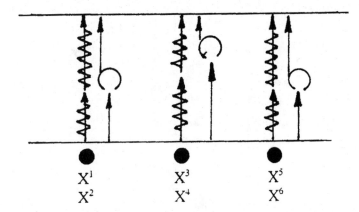

$$X^1 \qquad X^3 \qquad X^5$$
$$X^2 \qquad X^4 \qquad X^6$$

1. Players line up in pairs on the goal line.
2. The player at the front has a ball and dribbles slowly towards the half-way line. His partner follows closely behind.
3. Whenever he chooses, number one changes tempo and dribbles at speed to the half-way line.
4. Number two reacts to the change of tempo. He jumps in the air to head a ball, then sprints to the half-way line, attempting to get there first.
5. Players change roles after each sprint.

Variations
a) The player without the ball touches the ground with both hands before sprinting.
b) The player with the ball can choose whether to sprint for the half-way line or turn and sprint for the goal line.

SPEED AND AGILITY   PRACTICE 34

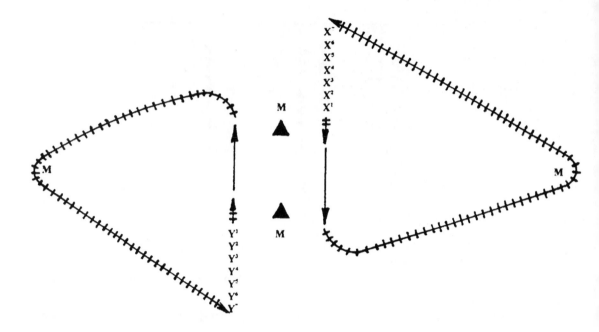

1. 2 cones are placed 18 yards apart and a marker is placed 2 yards from each cone.
2. Players line up in 2 lines, on either side of the markers.
3. X1 and Y1 start at the same time. They jog around the marker to the cone, then sprint to the cone opposite. At this point the next pair start.
4. After the sprint, the players peel off to their left, jog around the marker and join the back of their own line.
5. The relay continues for a set time or a set number of sprints.
6. This exercise will accommodate a large group of players.

Variations
a) Touch the ground by the marker, jog to the cone and sprint.
b) Jump in the air by the marker, jog to the cone and sprint.
c) Shuffle sideways between the marker and cone, then sprint.
d) Patter (short, quick steps) between the marker and cone, then sprint.
e) Run backwards to the cone, then sprint.
f) 2 tuck jumps between the marker and cone, then sprint.

SPEED AND AGILITY   **PRACTICE 35**

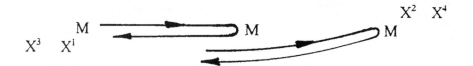

1. 3 markers are placed 10 yards apart. Players line up in 2 rows as shown in the diagram.
2. X1 starts and runs to the first marker and back, second marker and back and so on. He completes as many shuttles as possible in 15 seconds.
3. X2 starts and completes as many shuttles as possible in 15 seconds.
4. Players work one and rest 3.
5. The coach is responsible for the timing.

Variation
a) X1 sprints around the middle marker and back. As soon as he arrives back, X2 repeats the same action, then X3 and so on.
b) As above but players jump before sprinting.
c) Players touch the ground before sprinting.
d) Combine B and C.
e) Sprint to the marker, then run backwards to the line.
f) Face the opposite way, but turn to the right/left before sprinting.

SPEED AND AGILITY   **PRACTICE 36**

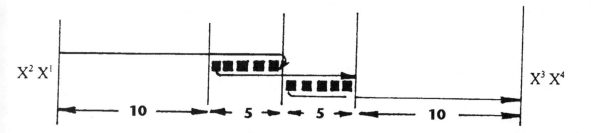

1. A 30 yard course is marked out as above. The players line up in 2 rows, facing each other.
2. X1 starts and sprints to the 15 yard line, runs backwards to the 10 yard line, forwards to the 20 yard line, backwards to the 15 yard line and forwards to the 30 yard line.
3. He hands over to X3, who repeats the same course.
4. Keep going for a set time or set number of sprints.

SPEED AND AGILITY **PRACTICE 37**

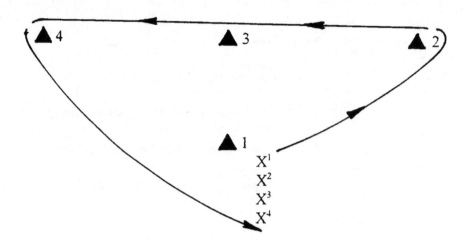

1. 4 cones are marked out, as in the diagram. 4 players form a line at cone 1.
2. X1 sprints around all 3 markers and joins the back of the line.
3. As soon as he arrives back, X2 starts and so on.
4. Repeat for a set time or number of sprints.

Variations

a) Work clockwise.
b) Jump in the air or touch the ground before sprinting.
c) Run to cone 2 and back, 3 and back, and 4 and back.
d) As above but run backwards to cone 1 each time.
e) Run to each cone and back, but do it in any order.
f) Run sideways facing inwards.
g) Run sideways facing outwards.

SPEED AND AGILITY   **PRACTICE 38**

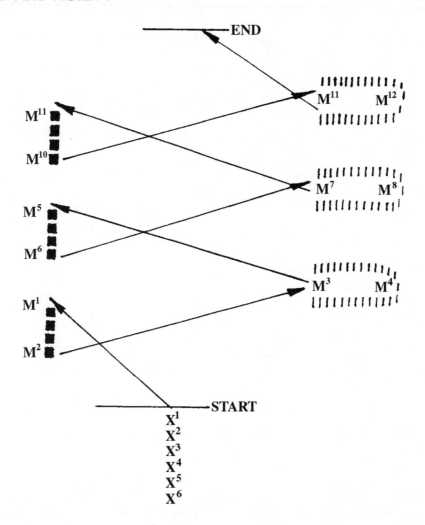

1. 12 markers are laid out, as in the diagram. The horizontal markers are 2 yards apart and vertical markers 4 yards apart.
2. X1 starts, sprints to M1 and runs backwards to M2.
3. He sprints across to the horizontal markers M3 and M4 and shuffles sideways around them.
4. He does the same on the rest of the course running backwards at the vertical markers and sideways at the horizontal ones.
5. X2 starts when X1 has reached M3.
6. When all runners have completed the course, X1 starts again from the opposite end.

SPEED AND AGILITY

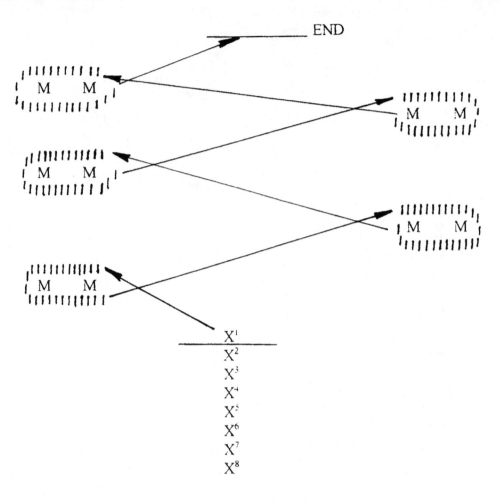

1. 10 markers are laid out as in the diagram. The sets of markers are 2 yards apart.
2. X1 starts and sprints to the front of the first set of markers. He shuffles sideways around them.
3. He repeats the same movements at all 5 sets, then sprints to the end line.
4. As soon as X1 has completed the first set of markers X2 starts.
5. Emphasize speed of movement around the markers.
6. When every body has completed the course, X1 starts again from the opposite end.

SPEED AND AGILITY   **PRACTICE 40**

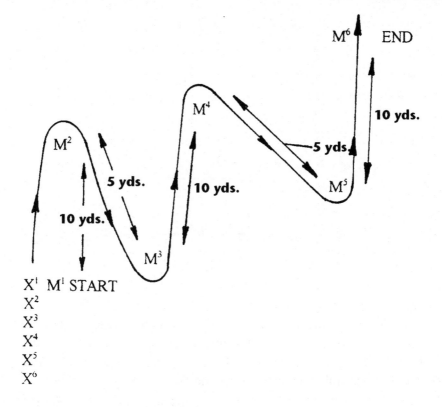

1. 6 markers are laid out as in the diagram. Total sprinting distance is 40 yards.
2. X1 starts and follows the course shown.
3. When he has reached M2, X2 starts.
4. When everybody has passed M6, the process starts again from the opposite end.

Variations
a) Players run backwards on the 5 yard sections.
b) X1 runs to M2, back to M1, then follows the same course as before. X2 does not start
   until X1 reaches M2 for the second time.

SPEED AND AGILITY   **PRACTICE 41**

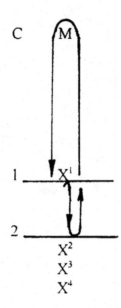

1. X1 starts on line 1, facing the coach, who is 10 yards away holding a ball.
2. When the coach drops the ball, X1 turns, touches line 2 with his right hand, turns again, touches line 1 with his left hand, then sprints around the marker and back.
3. X2 does not start until the coach drops the ball.

Variations
a) Touch line 2 with left hand and line 1 with right hand.
b) Touch each line with both hands.
c) Turn and jump in the air on line 2, turn again and jump in the air on line 1, then sprint around the marker and back.
d) Turn, sit down and up on line 2, turn again, sit down and up on line 1, then sprint around the marker and back.

SPEED AND AGILITY   **PRACTICE 42**

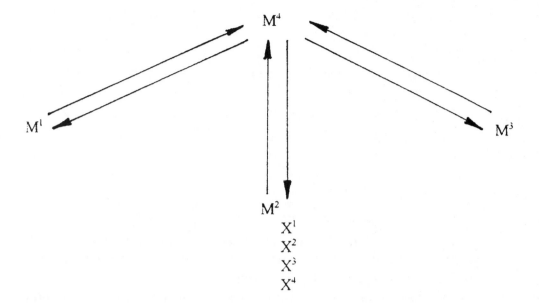

1. 4 players line up as in the diagram. All the markers are 10 yards apart.
2. X1 starts and sprints to M4, then to M1 and back, M3 and finally returns to M2.
3. X2 then starts and the process is continuous.
4. All the markers must be touched by hand.

Variation
Sprint out to M4, but run backwards to M1, M3 and M2.

SPEED AND AGILITY   **PRACTICE 43**

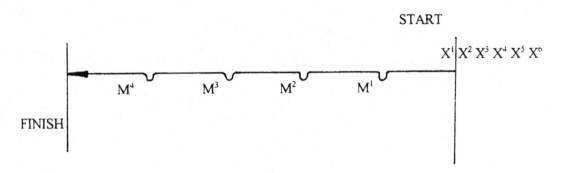

1. Players line up in a row facing 4 markers, which are 10 yards apart.
2. X1 sprints to the first marker, drops his left shoulder, moves back into an upright position, sprints to the second marker, drops his left shoulder, moves back into an upright position and so on. The same movement is carried out at each marker.
3. When X1 has reached the first marker, X2 starts.
4. When all runners have completed the course, X1 starts again from the other end.

Variations
a) Runners drop their right shoulder at each marker.
b) Runners drop their left, then right shoulder at each marker.
c) Runners slide right, two steps at the first marker, slide left, two steps at the second marker and so on.
d) Runners cut two steps at the first marker, cut two steps at the second marker and so on.
e) Runners cut two steps backwards and to the right at the first marker, cut two steps backwards and to the left at the second marker and so on.

SPEED AND AGILITY   **PRACTICE 44**

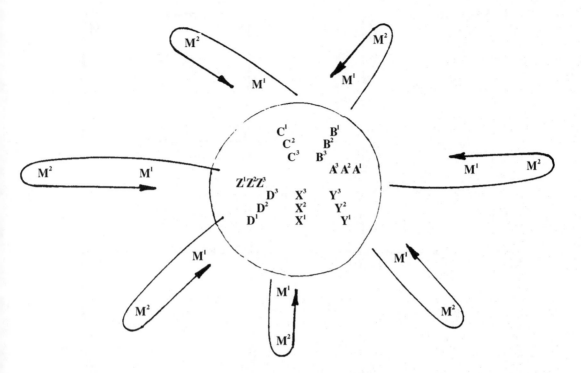

The above set-up offers a pattern that can be adopted safely with a large group. Players work outwards from a circle. The markers are 8 yards apart.

1. Players line up in several rows on the inside of a circle.
2. The 1s start, sprint around M2, then hand over to the 2s and so on.
3. The exercise is continuous and can last for a set time or certain number of sprints.

Variations

a) Players shuttle to M1 and back, M2 and back.
b) Players jump to head a ball at M1 and M2.
c) Players sprint to M1, run backwards to M2, then sprint home.
d) Players change the tempo by sprinting to M1, jogging to M2, sprinting back to M1, then jogging to rejoin the line.
e) Players touch the ground with both hands at M1 and M2.

SPEED AND AGILITY

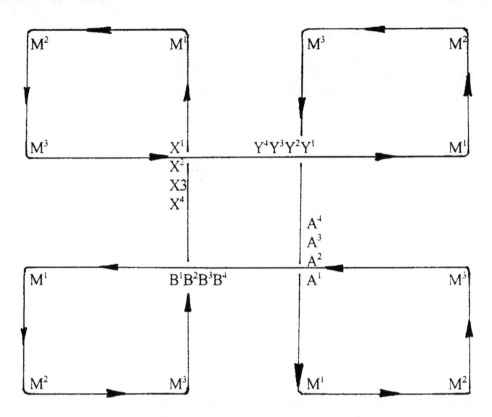

The above set-up offers a pattern that can be adopted safely with large groups. Players work outwards from a square.

1. Players line up in 4 rows on the inside of a square.
2. The 1s start, sprint around the square and hand over to the 2s and so on.
3. The exercise is continuous and can work on time or a set number of sprints.

Variations

a) Players sprint the other way around (M3 first).
b) Players shuffle to M1, M2 and M3 and back.
c) Players sprint around the square and back.
d) The 1s sprint around to M3 and patter on the spot. The 2s sprint to M3 and patter on the spot, while the 1s rejoin the back of their line.

SPEED AND AGILITY

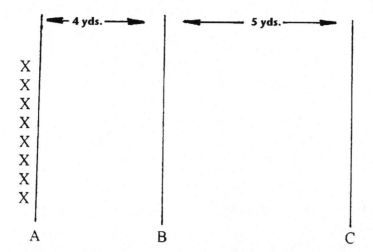

Patters – short, quick, shuffling steps over 4 yards. The arms must go as quickly as the legs and the body must be kept upright.

1. Players start on line A, patter to line B and sprint to line C and back.
2. Players patter to line B, jump in the air and sprint to C and back.
3. Players patter to line B, touch the ground with both hands and sprint to C and back.
4. Players patter to line B, jump in the air and run backwards to line A.
5. Players patter backwards to B and sprint forwards to A.
6. Players patter to B, jump forwards, then sprint to C and back.
7. Players patter forwards to B and patter backwards to A.
8. Players start in various positions on line A, before carrying out any of the above exercises.

SPEED AND AGILITY   PRACTICE 47

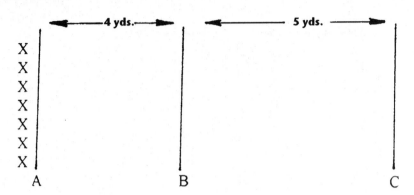

Ricochets – very small, quick, two footed jumps on the balls of the feet. The heels must not touch the ground.
1. Players start on line A, ricochet to line B and sprint to line C and back.
2. Players ricochet to line B, jump in the air and sprint to C and back.
3. Players ricochet to B, touch the ground with both hands and sprint to C and back.
4. Players ricochet to B, jump in the air and run backwards to A.
5. Players ricochet backwards to B and sprint forwards to A.
6. Players ricochet to B, jump forward, then sprint to C and back.
7. Players ricochet forwards to B and ricochet backwards to A.
8. Players start in various positions on line A before carrying out any of the above exercises.

SPEED AND AGILITY   PRACTICE 48

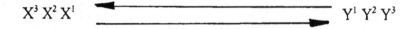

1. Players line up in 2 rows, facing each other, 20 yards apart.
2. X1 starts, sprints across and joins the back of the Y's line. As he arrives he shouts out "1".
3. Y1 sprints across to the X's, and joins the back of that line. As he arrives he shouts out "2" and so on.
4. Groups can compete against each other for a set time. A running total can be maintained using this system.

Variations
a) Vary the distance sprinted e.g. 5, 10, 15, 20, or 25 yards.
b) Adopt a variety of starting positions before each sprint.

SPEED AND AGILITY   **PRACTICE 49**

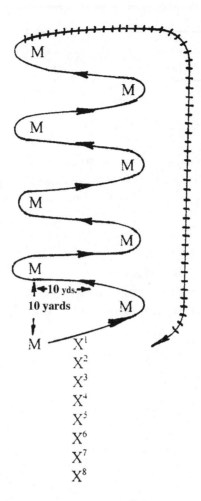

1. 9 markers are laid out as in the diagram. The players line up in a single file.
2. X1 starts and sprints the course shown. On reaching the last marker, he jogs back to the start.
3. X2 begins when X1 has reached the first marker.
4. Players work for a set time or a set number of sprints.
5. A variety of starting positions can be used, e.g. Sitting down, lying down, jumping in the air, touching the ground etc., before each sprint.

SPEED AND AGILITY   **PRACTICE 50**

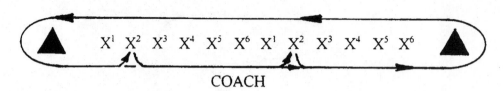

COACH

1. The players line up in a single line, facing the coach. A cone is placed at either end of the line.
2. Each player is given a number and one other player has the same number.
3. The coach shouts out a number (e.g.2) and both players sprint in a counter-clockwise direction around the group and cones and back to their place.

Variations
a) Players run in a clockwise direction.
b) More than one number is called at a time.
c) A third cone is placed behind the coach, which the players must run around.
d) Players begin in various starting positions, e.g. Sitting, facing the other way, lying down, kneeling etc.

SPEED AND AGILITY   **PRACTICE 51**

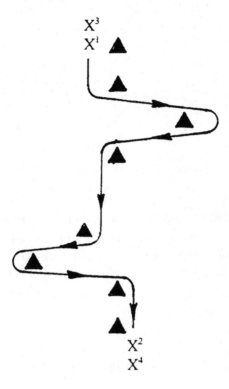

1. 8 cones are laid out, as in the above diagram.
2. 4 players line up facing each other in 2 lines and 25 yards apart.
3. X1 starts and sprints the course in the direction indicated.
4. He then joins the back of the opposite line and X2 sprints the course the other way.
5. Continue for a set time or set number of sprints.

Variation
Use a ball and dribble the course.

SPEED AND AGILITY   **PRACTICE 52**

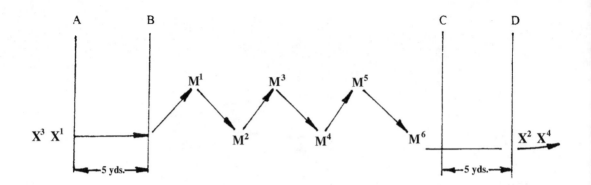

1. Players line up in 2 rows facing each other, 25 yards apart.
2. X1 starts and patters (short, quick steps) between lines A and B. He touches M1 with his left hand, M2 with his right hand and so on, until he has touched all 6 markers.
3. He then sprints between lines C and D before joining the back of the opposite line.
4. X2 patters between D and C, touches markers 1 and 6, sprints between B and A, then joins the back of the opposite line.

Variation
Players ricochet (very small, quick footed jumps on the balls of the feet) instead of patter.

SPEED AND AGILITY   **PRACTICE 53**

1. 11 markers are placed as in the diagram, with the wide markers 6 yards from the central line.
2. The players line up in 2 rows facing each other, 20 yards apart.
3. X1 starts, follows the course indicated and joins the back of the opposite line.
4. As soon as X1 finishes, X2 sprints the course in the opposite direction.
5. The exercise continues for a set time or set number of laps.

SPEED AND AGILITY   **PRACTICE 54**

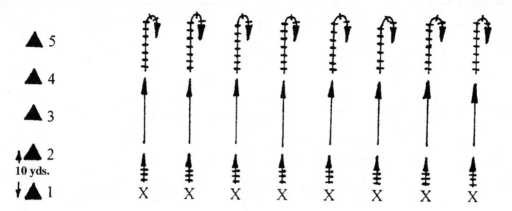

1. 5 cones are set out as markers 10 yards apart. Each has a number from 1 to 5.
2. All players start on marker 1 and jog to marker 5.
3. If the coach shouts out a number, the players sprint to that cone, then continue jogging.
4. On reaching marker 5, the players turn and jog back towards marker 1.
5. The coach must ensure the players change direction regularly e.g. as they jog towards marker 5, shout out 3.
6. Make sure recovery time is long enough, so that players maintain sprinting speed.

Variation
When the coach shouts out a number, the players jump in the air, touch the ground with both hands, sit down etc. before sprinting.

SPEED AND AGILITY   **PRACTICE 55**

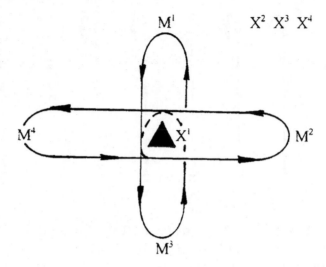

1. 4 markers are placed 6 yards from a central cone, as in the above diagram.
2. X1 starts at the middle cone and sprints to M1, back around the middle, continues on to M2, back around the middle cone to M3, back around the middle cone to M4, then back to the starting point.
3. Players should work in groups of 4, running one and resting 3.
4. Work for a set time or set number of sprints.

Variation
Sprint to the markers but run backwards to the middle cone.

SPEED AND AGILITY   **PRACTICE 56**

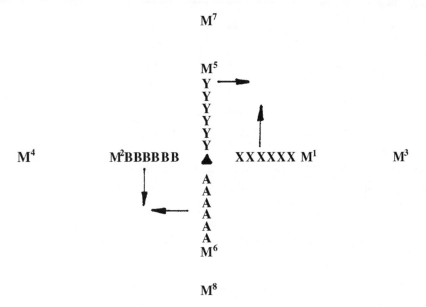

The above set-up offers a pattern that can be adopted safely with a large group. Players work outwards from the cross shape, in the direction indicated. ONE group goes at a time. The markers are 8 yards apart.

1. X's start and sprint to M5 and back, M7 and back.
2. Y's shuttle to M1 and back, M3 and back.
3. B's shuttle to M6 and back, M8 and back.
4. A's shuttle to M2 and back, M4 and back.

Variation

a) X's sprint to M5, M6, M7, M8.
b) Y's sprint to M1, M2, M3, M4.
c) B's sprint to M6, M5, M8, M7.
d) A's sprint to M2, M1, M4, M3.

SPEED AND AGILITY   **PRACTICE 57**

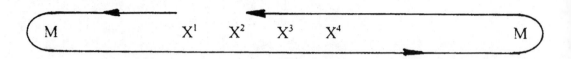

1. Players line up in teams of 4, between 2 markers placed 30 yards apart.
2. Each team has a baton or bib, which is exchanged every time a player completes a lap.
3. X1 starts and sprints the course indicated. He hands over to X2 and so on.
4. Work for a set time or set number of laps.

Variation
Run the course clockwise so that players turn to their right.

SPEED AND AGILITY   **PRACTICE 58**

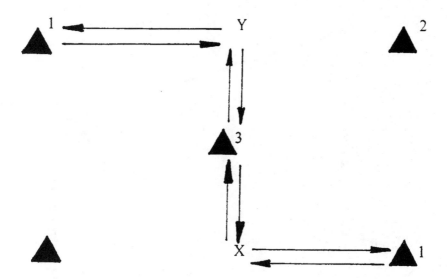

1. 5 cones are laid out as in the diagram. The starting positions for X and Y are 4 yards from each cone.
2. X and Y jog on the spot. The coach shouts out a number (i.e. 1,2 or 3). X and Y sprint to touch that cone, then return to their starting position and continue jogging.

Variations
a) Both players start with their back to cone 3.
b) The coach shouts out a number, but before sprinting the players perform a variety of exercises e.g. jump in the air, sit down, touch the ground with both hands, sprint on the spot etc.
c) Instead of calling a number, the coach shouts right, left or forward.
d) Players run sideways to each cone.
e) Players sprint to the cone, but run backwards to the starting point.

SPEED AND AGILITY **PRACTICE 59**

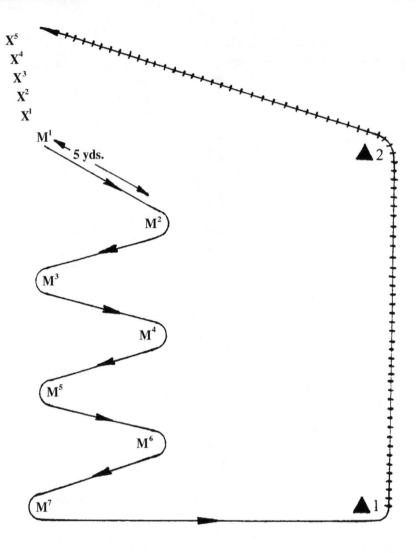

X⁵
X⁴
X³
X²
X¹

M¹
5 yds.
M²
M³
M⁴
M⁵
M⁶
M⁷

▲2
▲1

1. 7 markers are laid out as in the diagram, with cones 1 and 2 acting as the recovery zone. Players line up in single file.
2. X1 starts and sprints in and out of the markers, touching marker 1 with his left hand, marker 2 with his right hand and follows this pattern until he reaches marker 7.
3. He then sprints to cone 1 and jogs back to the start.

Variations
a) Players sprint to M2, run backwards to M3, sprint to M4, backwards to M5 and so on.
b) Players run around each marker before sprinting to the next one.

SPEED AND AGILITY   **PRACTICE 60**

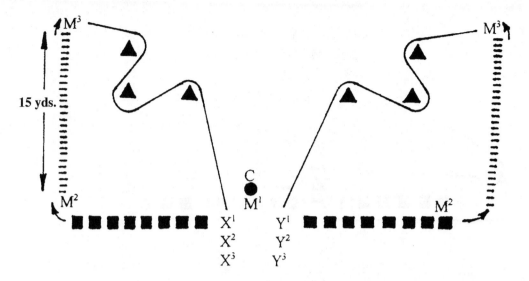

1. 2 players (X1 and Y1) stand facing each other at M1.
2. The exercise starts when the coach bounces a ball. Both players then run backwards to M2, sideways to M3 and in and out of the cones, before handing over to the next player in the team.
3. Work for a set time or set number of sprints.

Variations
a) Players perform various agility exercises such as touching the ground with both hands, jumping in the air, sitting down etc. before performing the run.
b) Players stand back to back at M1 and sprint the course when the coach gives the signal.
c) Players have a ball and dribble the course.
d) Players stand facing the coach. They run sideways to M2, backwards to M3, then sprint the rest of the course.

SPEED AND AGILITY   **PRACTICE 61**

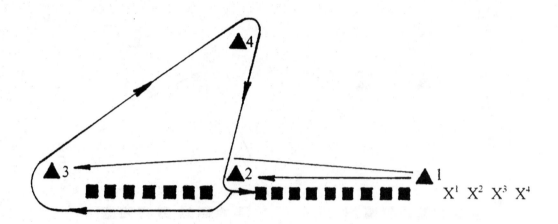

1. 4 cones are placed in a triangle shape, all 6 yards apart.
2. X1 starts, sprints to cone 2 and runs backwards to cone 1.
3. He then sprints to cone 3, runs backwards to cone 2 and forwards again to cone 3.
4. From here he sprints around cone 4 to cone 2, which he touches with his hand and then runs backwards to his starting position at cone 1.
5. Work for a set time or set number of runs.

Variations
a) The players shuttle to cone 2 and back, cone 3 and back and cone 4 and back.
b) The players run to cone 2, backwards to cone 1, forwards to cone 3, backwards to cone 1, forwards to cone 4, and back.
c) The players shuttle to cone 2 and back, cone 3 and back, then run around cones 4 and 3 and back to start.

SPEED AND AGILITY   **PRACTICE 62**

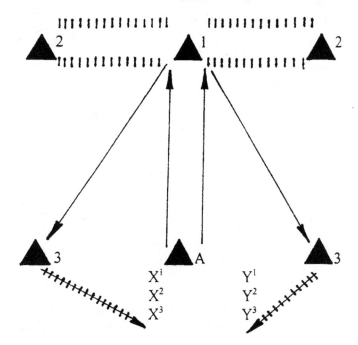

1. 6 cones are positioned as in the diagram. The distance from cone A to cone 1 is 20 yards and from cone 2, 5 yards.
2. X1 and Y1 start at the same time and sprint to cone 1. They then run to cone 2 and back to cone 1 sideways.
3. After touching cone 1, they sprint to cone 3, then rejoin the back of their line.
4. X2 and Y2 do not start until the coach gives the signal.
5. Work for a set time or set number of sprints.

Variations
a) X1 and Y1 have a ball each, dribble to cone 1 and leave it. They then run sideways to cone 2 and back, pass the ball to the next player in line, then sprint to cone 3 and join the back of their line.
b) As above but the players run backwards from cone 1 to cone 3.

SPEED AND AGILITY   **PRACTICE 63**

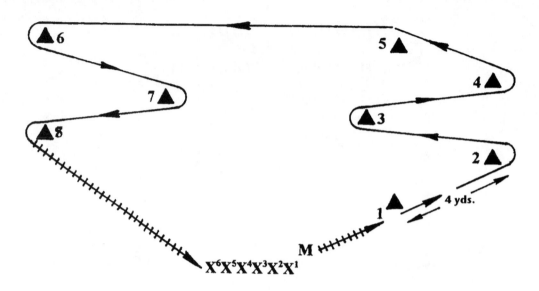

1. Players line up as in the diagram, with X1 approximately 4 yards from the first cone.
2. X1 jogs to cone 1 then ZIG-ZAGs through the "W" pattern at top speed. Emphasis is on fast foot plant and cut. X2 starts when X1 has reached the first cone.
3. X1 does a forward sprint of 17 yards between cones 5 and 6, performs a 180° turn between cones 7 and 8, then walks to the back of the line.

Variations
a) Run sideways through the "W" pattern with right foot leading.
b) Run sideways through the "W" pattern with left foot leading.
c) Run sideways through the "W" pattern with right foot leading between cones 1 and 2, left foot between cones 3 and 4 and so on.
d) Forwards to cone 2, backwards to cone 3 and so on.
e) Spin behind cones 2, 3 and 4.

Emphasis must be on a quick change of direction at each turn, with a quick hip motion on each section.

SPEED AND AGILITY   **PRACTICE 64**

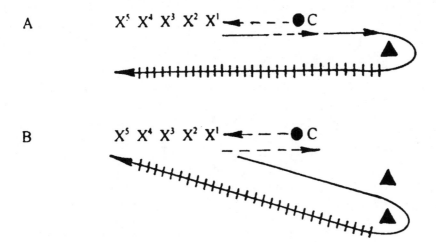

1. 5 or more players line up as in the diagram, with X1 approximately 4 yards from the coach.
2. The coach passes the ball to X1, who passes it back first time. X1 then sprints to the cone, which is 6 yards beyond the coach and jogs to the back of the group.
3. As soon as X1 has sprinted, the coach passes to X2, who repeats the same drill.
4. Players should concentrate on acceleration and the drive from their first step.

Variations
a) Players head the ball back to the coach before sprinting.
b) Players volley the ball back to the coach before sprinting.
c) Players pass the ball, then cut back 2 steps before sprinting.
d) Players make a curved run to the cone.
e) Players do all the above but at an angle. See diagram B.

SPEED AND AGILITY   **PRACTICE 65**

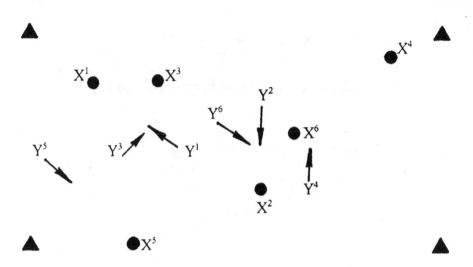

1. A 30 yard by 30 yard grid is marked out with 4 cones. Any number of players can work in the grid.
2. Players are divided into pairs, with one ball for each pair. In the diagram, Y's are the working players and X's have the ball.
3. Y's position themselves between 10 and 15 yards from their partners. When ready, they sprint to their partners, play a 1 / 2, then stop where they are.
4. X's then dribble to another area of the grid. When they have fully recovered, Y's sprint again to play a 1 / 2 with their partners.
5. Y's must concentrate on the drive from their first 5 steps. Also, with so many pairs, it is unlikely that they will be able to sprint in a straight line.
6. Work for 1 minute, then change roles.

Variations
The sprinting player starts:
a) On one knee.
b) In a press-up position but with one hand off the ground.
c) Sitting on the ground.
d) Lying face down.
e) Lying face down, then rolls over and gets up.

SPEED AND AGILITY   **PRACTICE 66**

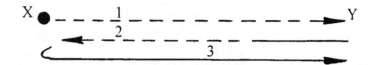

1. X and Y stand 10 yards apart. X starts with the ball while Y is the working player.
2. X passes to Y who returns the ball first time and follows his pass.
3. Y touches his feet on top of the ball, which X has under control. He toe taps the ball 3 times then sprints back to his place.
4. The process starts again with roles reversed.
5. Emphasis should be on speed of acceleration after passing the ball and the quickness of the turn.

Variations
a) The resting player holds the ball at various heights for the working player to kick or head.

b) After touching the ball, the working player:
    1)   Steps back, turns and sprints.
    2)   Runs backwards.
    3)   Runs sideways, feet remaining at shoulder width apart.
    4)   Does a double cut, right then left.
    5)   Carriocas

c) The drill can be used as a speed endurance session if a player works for one minute before changing roles.

SPEED AND AGILITY   PRACTICE 67

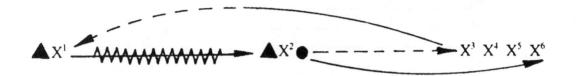

1. 6 or more players line up as in the diagram. The distance between X1 and X2 is 14 yards and X2 and X3, 5 yards.
2. X2 starts with the ball, passes to X3 and sprints to the back of the group.
3. X3 passes to X1 and sprints to X1's position.
4. X1 dribbles at speed to X2's position, passes to X4 and the sequence starts again.

Variations
a) X3 chips the ball to X1 and follows his pass.
b) X3 runs in an arc.
c) X3 takes 2 touches before passing.
d) X2 throws the ball for X3 to head or volley before sprinting.
e) After passing the ball, X3 jumps in the air, runs backwards 3 steps, hops twice, bounds twice, etc. before sprinting.

SPEED AND AGILITY   PRACTICE 68

1. 3 or more players line up as in the diagram. Two cones are placed 10 yards apart.
2. X1 starts with the ball, passes to X2 and follows his pass.
3. X2 receives the ball with the outside of his right foot, takes it to the other side of the cone, passes to X3 and follows his pass.
4. X3 receives the ball with the outside of his right foot, takes it to the other side of the cone, passes to X1 and follows his pass.
5. Players must concentrate on 'exploding' during the first 5 steps after passing the ball.

Variations
a) Work the other side of the cone so that players take the ball with the outside of the left foot.
b) Pass the ball and sprint in an arc.
c) Receive the ball with the inside of the left foot and pass with the right.
d) Receive the ball with the inside of the right foot and pass with the left.

SUMMARY

1. The aim of this type of training is to increase the ability to recognize what is required in a given situation, then react quickly to that stimulus. It is important that the correct motor units are recruited in order to produce the maximum force in the shortest possible time.

2. The training program must be designed to encompass the ability to start quickly from different positions, make rapid changes in direction, reach top speed as quickly as possible and stop rapidly but retain balance.

3. This type of training can be divided into two: **quickness**, which involves recognition and reaction, the first 5 steps, and **speed**, which occurs once the player has completed the first 5 steps. Quickness is more important than speed in most soccer situations.

4. In training it is essential to differentiate between stationary starts and starts with forward motion, since the former requires sufficient strength to overcome gravity. If a player is weak on his first step, then the extra power training is required.

5. Stationary starts and flying starts must be incorporated within the framework of soccer-related actions. It is usually best to combine coordination exercises with an explosive short sprint.

6. All speed training should be done at the start of the session, immediately after the warm up.

7. Players must perform this work maximally and the rest periods should be long enough for muscles to recover fully.

8. "You cannot run fast by training slow." If the body is made to move faster, the muscles learn to react faster and it becomes a habit. Some speed, quickness or agility work should therefore take place in EVERY training session.

9. In the development of the nervous system, the hands develop earlier than the feet. Therefore, from about the age of 8, children should do suitable footwork exercises which stimulate frequency of movement. This should occur in a playful environment of relays, tag games and specific coordination exercise.

10. Speed training must be functional and related to movements in the game.

SPEED ENDURANCE TRAINING

Bill Shankly, when manager at Huddersfield Town, allowed Derek Ibbotson, a sub 4 minute miler, to train with the players. "Ibbo was finished in half an hour at our 5-a-sider" Shankly said, "You've got to be fit for soccer, not running miles." Shankly rightly observed, all those years ago, that training has to be sport specific.

Since that time, the demands of soccer have grown. There are now a number of countries participating and this has led to an increase in level and intensity of competition. With higher standards of performance required, it has been necessary to increase the level of training.

With this in mind, Bangsbo measured top class Danish players and found that they produced high blood lactate levels during a game, and so recommended that the lactate producing energy pathways should be specifically trained. Speed endurance training, however, is very demanding and should only be used at the end of a training session, as the players will be physically affected for some time afterwards.

For this type of training, players should work maximally for between 30 to 45 seconds, so that extreme acidification does not occur. It is crucial that they perform similar movements to those of a match, so high intensity games or drills with a ball are best. If facilities are lacking and it is not possible to use a ball, then shuttle run type activities can be used, as they simulate the changes of direction and running patterns of a game. The shuttle can be made even more realistic and demanding by having players sit down, touch the ground with one hand or jump to head a ball.

Further research by Bangsbo, Agnevik and Dr. Luc Van Agt has also found that players from lower leagues produce considerably less lactate than top class players. It is therefore recommended that speed endurance training should have a low priority with all but elite players, since this training is both physically and mentally demanding and is only used to a limited degree by most soccer players during a game. When semi-professional and amateur players have limited time available for practice, it makes sense to use the time more effectively on other forms of training. For players under 16, this type of training should not be used at all.

The aims of this type of training are clearly to improve the player's ability to recover more quickly after high intensity exercise. The following 29 exercises can be used and adapted according to the ability of the players being trained.

SPEED ENDURANCE AND AGILITY   PRACTICE 1

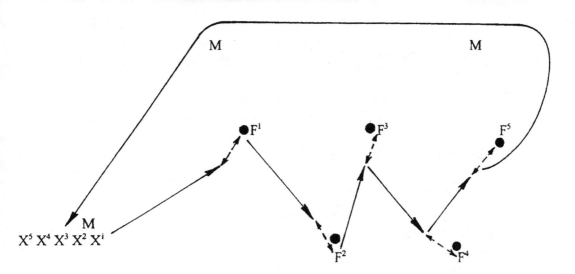

1. 10 players line up as in the diagram. The feeders have a ball each and are 20 yards apart.
2. X1 sprints to F1, plays a 1 / 2, sprints across to F2, plays a 1 / 2 and so on.
3. After playing a 1 / 2 with each feeder, X1 sprints around the markers and back to the starting position.
4. Once X1 has passed the ball back to F1, X2 starts.
5. Players complete a lap rest for 35 seconds, then repeat the course.
6. The runners and feeders change positions after 6 sprints.

SPEED ENDURANCE AND AGILITY   PRACTICE 2

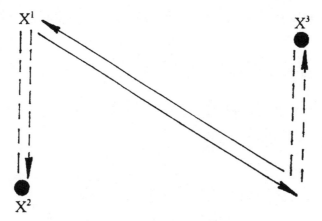

1. 3 players line up as in the diagram. X2 and X3 have a ball each. X1 is the working player.
2. X1 receives a pass from X2, returns it first time then sprints the diagonal.
3. As he arrives, he receives a pass from X3, which he returns first time then sprints the diagonal.
4. X1 works for a minute then changes place with X2.

SPEED ENDURANCE AND AGILITY   **PRACTICE 3**

1. X1 and X2 stand facing each other about 5 yards apart.
2. They pass the ball to each other, but after each pass, sit down and get up again as quickly as possible.
3. Work for a minute, then rest for a minute.

SPEED ENDURANCE AND AGILITY   **PRACTICE 4**

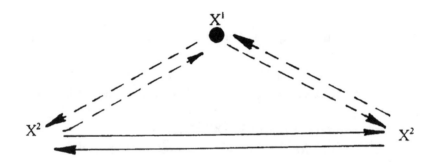

1. The players take up the positions as in the diagram. X1 is standing with the ball and X2 is sitting.
2. X1 sends alternate passes to the right or left, which X2 must run to and return.
3. After passing the ball back to X1, who remains stationary, X2 must sit down and get up again quickly.
4. This is a strenuous exercise, so players should change roles regularly.

SPEED ENDURANCE AND AGILITY   **PRACTICE 5**

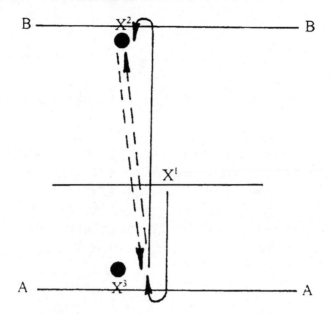

1. 3 players line up as in the diagram. X2 and X3 have a ball each and are 20 yards apart. X1 is the working player and starts on the middle line.
2. He sprints to line A, turns, receives a pass from X2, returns it first time, then sprints to line B.
3. He turns, receives a pass from X3, returns it first time, then sprints to line A.
4. X1 works for one minute then changes places with X2.
5. See which player completes the most shuttles in one minute.

SPEED ENDURANCE AND AGILITY   **PRACTICE 6**

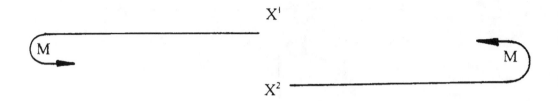

1. 2 players line up opposite each other between 2 markers, which are 15 yards apart. One (X2) is designated the catcher and the other (X1) the runner.
2. The players run in the direction indicated, with X2 chasing X1.
3. At anytime, the coach may call a change in direction. The roles of the players are immediately reversed and X1 becomes the catcher and X2 the runner.
4. The more changes in direction, the harder the exercise.
5. Players work for 40-60 seconds, then rest.

Variation
The exercise can be made more difficult by changing the way the players move, e.g. hopping, running backwards, two-footed jumps, etc.

SPEED ENDURANCE AND AGILITY   PRACTICE 7

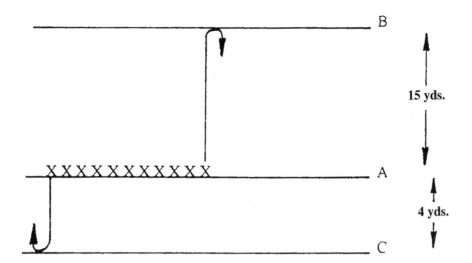

1. Players work for 10 to 30 seconds. The REST PERIOD is the same as the work period.
2. Players line up on line A and sprint to line B and back for 20 seconds.
3. They jog on the spot for 20 seconds, then shuttle between A and C for 15 seconds.
4. They jog on the spot for 15 seconds, then work again under the instruction of the coach.

Variations
a) Shuttle between A and B, but head a ball at B.
b) Shuttle between A and B, but volley a ball left and right at B.
c) Shuttle between A and C, but run backwards to A each time.
d) Shuttle between A and C, but sit down at C.
e) Shuttle between A and B with the coach shouting out changes of direction during the shuttle.
f) Players patter (short, quick steps) between A and C.
g) Players ricochet (very small, quick, 2 footed jumps on the balls of the feet) between A and C.

SPEED ENDURANCE AND AGILITY   PRACTICE 8

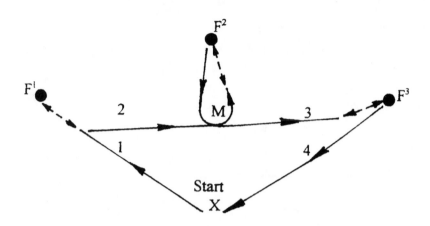

1. 4 players line up as in the diagram. F1, F2, and F3 are feeders, have a ball each, and are 20 yards from the marker. X is the working player.
2. X sprints to F1, plays a 1 / 2 with him, turns, sprints around the marker to F2, plays a 1/2 with him, sprints around the marker to F3, plays a 1/2 with him, sprints back to his starting position and the practice continues.
3. X works for 1 minute then changes places with one of the feeders.

Variation
The working player goes to F3 first, then F2 and finally F1.

SPEED ENDURANCE AND AGILITY   PRACTICE 9

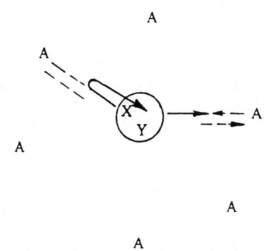

1. 6 players, each with a ball, form a circle approximately 25 – 30 yards across.
2. Another small circle, 2/3 yards across is made in the middle with markers or chalk.
3. Players X and Y start in the small circle, with X the attacker and Y the defender.
4. X runs to any player in the circle, calls for the ball and passes it back first time.
5. Y tries to intercept the pass.
6. As soon as X has returned the ball, both he and Y move quickly back to the starting circle and the process starts again.
7. If Y intercepts the ball, X remains the attacking player.
8. The pair work for 60 seconds and are then replaced by another pair.
9. When the pair enter the circle a second time, the roles are reversed.

Variations
a) 6 players form a circle, 3 of whom have a ball. When X calls and receives the ball, he passes it to a free player in the circle.
b) If it is a large group e.g. 12 players or more, 2 pairs can work at the same time.

SPEED ENDURANCE AND AGILITY

PRACTICE 10

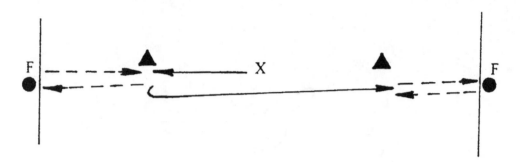

1. Players work in teams of 3. 2 players line up 25 yards apart and have a ball each. A marker is placed 5 yards away from each of these players.
2. The active player starts in the middle and sprints towards one of the feeders. When the runner reaches the 5 yard mark, the feeder passes to the runner, who returns the ball first time.
3. The runner then turns and sprint across to the other feeder and when he reaches the 5 yard mark, the sequence is repeated.
4. The runner works for a set time or set number of runs, then the roles are changed.

Variations
a) The runner has 2 touches.
b) The ball is headed back to the feeder.
c) The ball is volleyed back to the feeder.
d) The ball is half-volleyed back to the feeder.
e) The runner has 3 touches.
f) The ball is controlled on the chest, then volleyed back to the feeder.

SPEED ENDURANCE AND AGILITY

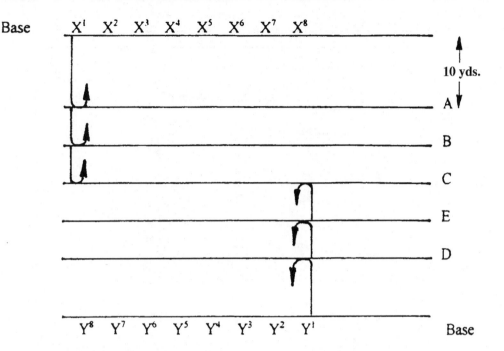

1. 7 lines are drawn, 10 yards apart.
2. X's and Y's line up on the base lines.
3. X1 and Y1 start at the same time and X1 sprints to A and back, B and back, C and back, while Y1 sprints to D and back, E and back, C and back.
4. As soon as X1 reaches A and Y1 reaches D, X2 and Y2 start.
5. The aim is to catch the person in front.
6. X1 and Y1 rest until everybody in their line gets back, then the process starts again.
7. Work for a set time or set numbers of shuttles.

Variation

All players start on line C and then follow the same pattern as above. X1 and Y1 start – X1 sprints to B and back, A and back, base line and back, while Y1 sprints to E and back, D and back, base line and back.

SPEED ENDURANCE AND AGILITY

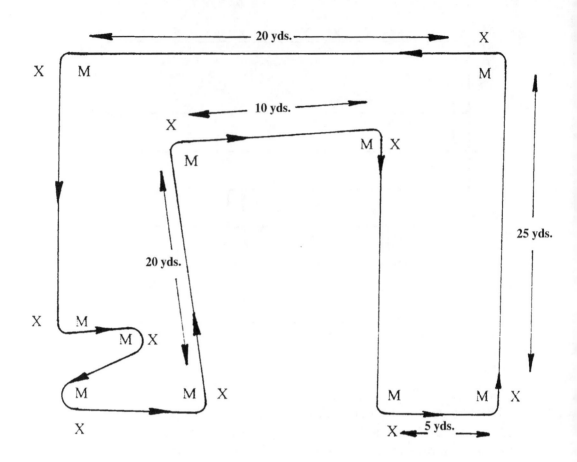

1. 10 marks are placed as in the diagram and one player starts at each marker.
2. On a signal from the coach, the players sprint 2 laps of the course, in the direction indicated.
3. The aim is to complete the course as quickly as possible and overtake other players.

Variations
a) Run the course for a set time, but change direction on a signal from the coach.
b) Put hurdles and hoops on designated sections of the course.
c) Use a ball and dribble 2 laps.
d) Dribble one lap, sprint to the other.
e) On a signal from the coach, do two footed jumps over the ball.

SPEED ENDURANCE AND AGILITY

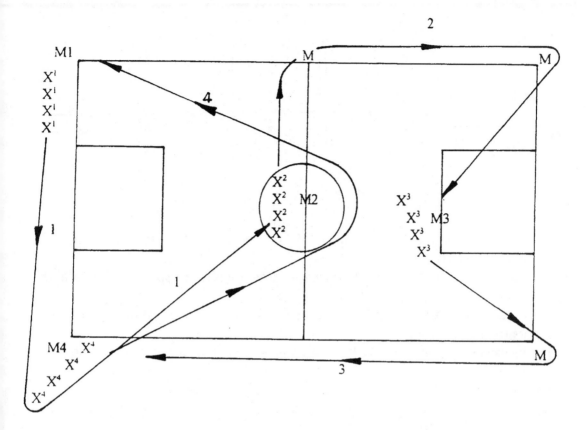

1. 7 cones are laid out on a soccer field, as shown in the above diagram.
2. The players are divided into 4 groups and each group is given a number from 1 to 4.
3. The groups start on their corresponding number and sprint the legs shown. X1s for example start at M1, sprint behind the goal and finish the leg at the cone in the center circle, which the X2's started from. Their second leg will follow the X2's course and finish on the edge of the penalty area.
4. All groups start at the same time on each leg. A different runner leads every time.
5. At the end of each leg, players get 40 seconds rest.
6. Each group completes 2 laps of the course. This will involve 8 sprints.

SPEED ENDURANCE AND AGILITY   PRACTICE 14

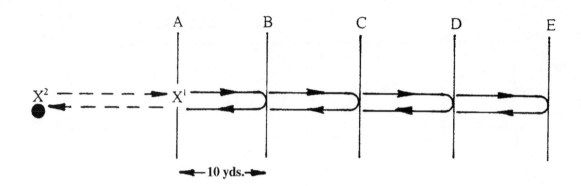

1. 5 lines are marked out 10 yards apart. X1 stands on line A while his partner, X2, faces him 10 yards away.
2. X2 plays the ball to X1, who returns it first time, then turns, sprints to line B and back to line A.
3. Just as he arrives, X2 plays the next ball in, which is returned first time. X1 then sprints to line C and back.
4. The process continues until X1 has visited all 4 lines. The players then change roles.

Variation
X1 starts with his back to X2 each time and only turns on his partner's signal.

SPEED ENDURANCE AND AGILITY

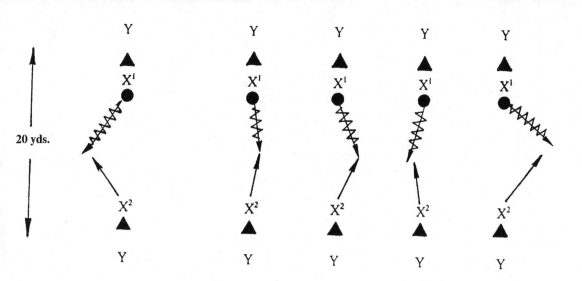

20 yds.

1. Any number of cones are laid out, 20 yards apart. There must be one cone per player.
2. X1 starts with the ball and attempts to strike his partner's cone. He dribbles, changes tempo, dummies, etc. in order to beat his opponent.
3. If X2 wins the ball, the roles are reversed and X1 must defend his own cone.
4. The ball is never dead and the players are not restricted to any area.
5. Players must work strenuously for 90 seconds, then change with a resting pair (Y's).

SPEED ENDURANCE AND AGILITY   **PRACTICE 16**

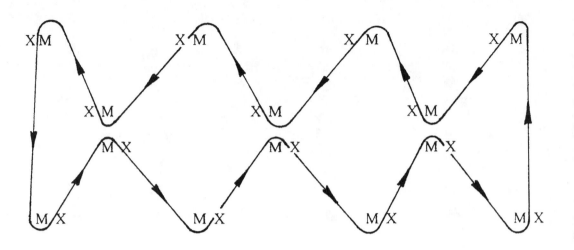

1. 14 markers are laid out as in the above diagram.
2. A runner stands at each marker and on a signal from the coach sprints the course in the direction shown, until he is back to his original position.
3. Runners should sprint one lap and rest two.

Variations
a) Run the course in the opposite direction.
b) Dribble the course.
c) Sit down, jump in the air, touch the ground with both hands, change direction, etc. as instructed by the coach.
d) Sprint two laps.

SPEED ENDURANCE AND AGILITY

PRACTICE 17

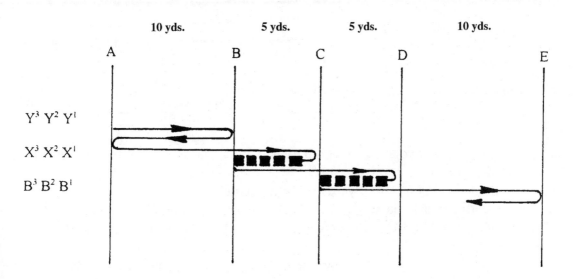

1. A course is marked out as shown in the above diagram.
2. The 1's start and sprint to line B and back, run backwards to C and back to B, run backwards to D and back to C, then to E and back to line A and hand over.
3. The players work for a set time or set number of shuttles.

Variations
a) Use a ball and dribble the same course.
b) Time the players and when there is a 20% drop off in performance, eliminate those who fail to meet the target time.

SPEED ENDURANCE AND AGILITY   **PRACTICE 18**

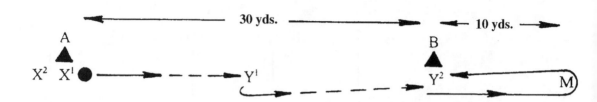

1. 3 players line up on two cones, A and B, which are 30 yards apart. A fourth player (Y1) starts in the middle.
2. 2 more markers are placed 10 yards beyond each cone.
3. X1 starts with the ball, passes to Y1, follows his pass and takes Y1's place.
4. On receiving the ball, Y1 turns, passes to Y2, sprints around the marker and waits at cone B.
5. Y2 passes to X1, follows his pass and takes X1's place. X1 turns, passes to X2, sprints around the marker and waits at cone A.
6. It is important that there are only 4 players per group, in order to maintain the intensity of the exercise.

SPEED ENDURANCE AND AGILITY

PRACTICE 19

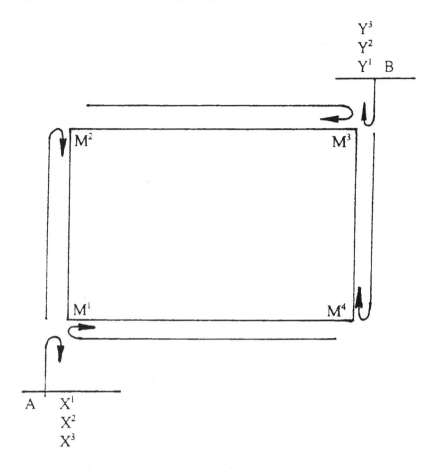

1. 2 groups of players line up as in the diagram, on the opposite sides of a 15 yard square and 10 yards from the nearest marker.
2. X1 and Y1 start at the same time. X1 sprints to M1 and back to A. Y1 sprints to M3 and back to B.
3. When all the runners have completed the same shuttle, X1 then works to M2 and back, while Y1 works to M4 and back.
4. The shuttles are gradually increased and on the final run, the X's sprint 4 sides of the square to M1 and back, while Y's sprint 4 sides of the square to M3 and back.
5. Work for a set time or set number of shuttles.

SPEED ENDURANCE AND AGILITY   PRACTICE 20

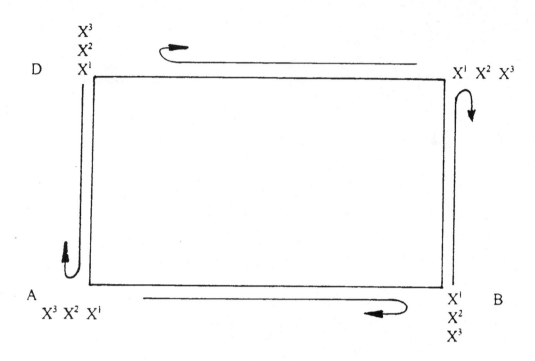

1. 4 groups of players line up on the corners of a 20 yard square.
2. All the 1's start at the same time and sprint one side of the square and back
   (e.g. line A sprints to B and back.)
3. This is repeated by the other players in the group.
4. The 1's then sprint two sides of the square and back e.g. A will sprint to C and back.
5. The process continues with players sprinting 3 sides of the square and back, then 4
   sides and back.
6. The exercise continues for a set time or number of complete laps.

Variation
Players sprint 2 sides then run diagonally across the square to their group. They must be careful to avoid other players.

SPEED ENDURANCE AND AGILITY

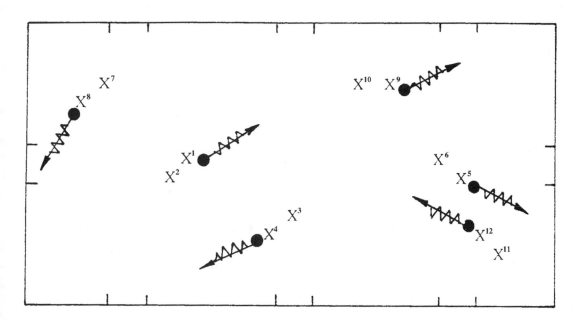

1. A field is marked out as in the above diagram, with several goals a yard wide and placed at regular intervals around the area.
2. The players work in pairs, with one ball between two.
3. One of the pair has the ball and tries to score in any of the goals, while his partner attempts to gain possession and score himself.
4. If a player scores, he keeps possession but cannot return to the goal he has scored in until he has attacked another goal.
5. The practice continues for 2 minutes and the partner at the end with the most goals wins.
6. Players then change partners and the exercise is repeated.

SPEED ENDURANCE AND AGILITY

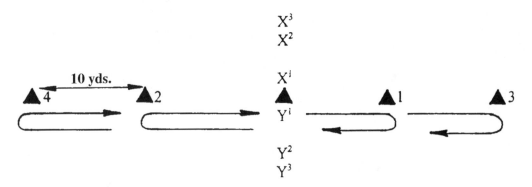

1. 5 cones are set out 10 yards apart.
2. X1 and Y1 start at the same time and sprint to cone 1. Here they jump in the air to head a ball, turn and sprint to cone 2.
3. At cone 2 they touch the ground with one hand, turn and sprint to cone 3.
4. They jump in the air to head a ball, turn and sprint to cone 4.
5. At cone 4 they touch the ground with one hand, turn and sprint back to the start, where they hand over to X2 and Y2.
6. Players work for a set time or set number of shuttles.

Variations
a) Players sit down instead if heading a ball.
b) X's work in the opposite direction to Y's. Thus X1 visits cone 1 and Y1 visits cone 2 first.

SPEED ENDURANCE AND AGILITY

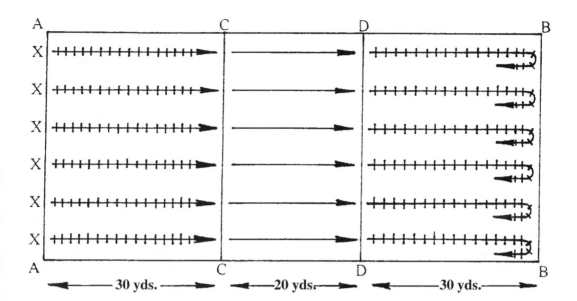

1. The group starts together from line A and jogs to C.
2. They sprint the 20 yard section to D, then jog to B.
3. On the return, the runners jog to D, shuttle 3 times between D and C, then jog to B.
4. The runners jog to C, shuttle 5 times between D and C, then jog to B.
5. The action is repeated with 7 shuttles, 9 shuttles, 11 shuttles between jogs.
6. Once the group has reached 11 shuttles, they come back down the clock with 9,7,5,3 and 1 shuttle(s).

Variation

Before each sprint, players can be instructed to jump in the air, sit down, touch the ground with both hands, etc.

SPEED ENDURANCE AND AGILITY   PRACTICE 24

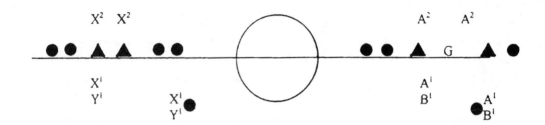

1. A small field is set up on one third of a soccer field.
2. 2 players from each team take turns and in each game perform man to man marking.
3. The teams defend one goal and attack the other.
4. A large supply of balls should be available in order to avoid delays and to ensure the game is played at a high intensity.
5. Players work for 1 to 2 minutes and rest the same.
6. The game is more realistic if full size goals and 2 goalkeepers are used.

SPEED ENDURANCE AND AGILITY   **PRACTICE 25**

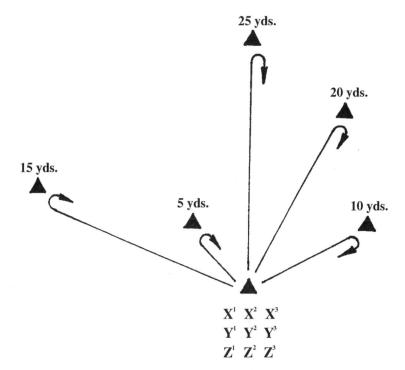

X¹ X² X³
Y¹ Y² Y³
Z¹ Z² Z³

1. 5 markers are laid out as in the above diagram.
2. X's start at the same time and work from left to right.
3. X1 runs to 15 yds and back, 25 yds and back and 10 yds and back.
4. X2 starts on the 25 yd line and finishes on the 5 yd shuttle.
5. Y's start when all the X's finish and Z's start when all the Y's finish.
6. Work for a set number of shuttles.

SPEED ENDURANCE AND AGILITY   **PRACTICE 26**

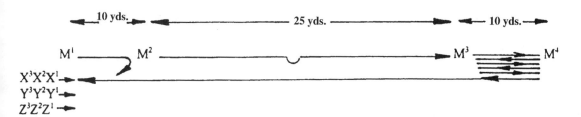

1. 4 markers are set out as in the above diagram.
2. Players work in groups of 3. The 1's start.
3. They sprint to M2, back to M1, then sprint to M3. Somewhere between M2 and M3 the runners must sit down and get up again.
4. They shuttle 6 times between M3 and M4, then sprint back to the start and hand over to the 2's and so on.
5. Work for a set time or set number of shuttles.
6. Other agility exercises can be performed between M2 and M3, at the direction of the coach.

SPEED ENDURANCE AND AGILITY PRACTICE 27

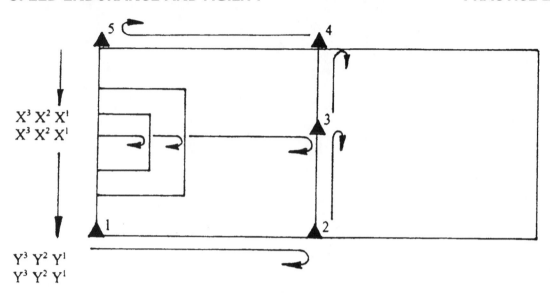

1. 5 cones are set out on half a field, as shown in the diagram, with 1 on each corner flag, 2 on the half-way line and 1 in the center circle.
2. The center backs and strikers (X's) work the center of the field and shuttle to the 6 yard line and back, 18 yard line and back, and half-way line and back. Every player completes the 6 yard run before moving on to the next shuttle.
3. The mid-field players and full backs (Y's) work on the longer shuttles around half a field. They work to cone 2 and back, cone 3 and back, cone 4 and back, cone 5 and back, then complete 1 half lap. All runners complete each shuttle before moving on to the next one.
4. The Y's are the timing group and X's work until Y's finish.

SPEED ENDURANCE AND AGILITY   **PRACTICE 28**

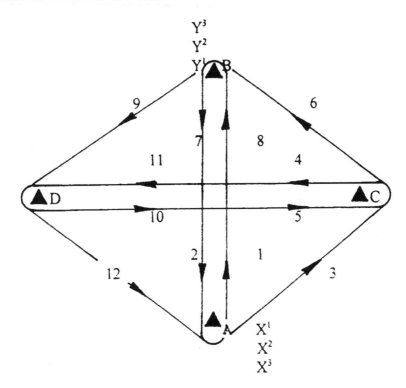

This figure illustrates the course run by X's. Y's meanwhile run the course in the following order:
2, 1, 9, 10, 11, 12, 1, 2, 3, 4, 5, 6.

1. 2 groups of players line up facing each other, as in the diagram. Cones A, B, C and D are 15 yards apart and form a cross.
2. X1 and Y1 start on the right hand side of their cone, sprint around the cone in front of them and back to their starting position.
3. They then run to the cone on their right and sprint around cones C and D.
4. Both players work their way around the cross until all 4 runs have been completed, then they hand over to X2 and Y2. However, X2 and Y2 do not start until the coach gives the signal.
5. Work for a set time or set number of shuttles.

SPEED ENDURANCE AND AGILITY   PRACTICE 29

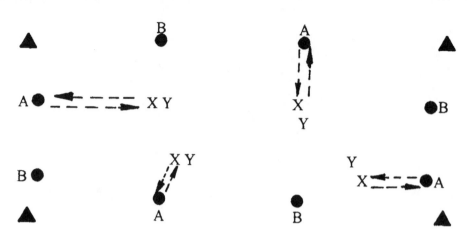

1. 12 to 24 players can participate in this exercise.
2. A grid 35 yds by 25 yds is marked out with 4 cones.
3. Players with the ball are placed on the outside of the grid, as shown in the diagram. They are support players.
4. The other players pair off inside the grid. One of the pair is designated the attacker and the other the defender. All the attacking players must wear a bib.
5. The attacking players must get free of their defenders, receive a ball from any support player and play it back first time.
6. The attackers count the number of passes they can make in 40 seconds.
7. Those on the outside then change places with those on the inside.

Variations
a)   Attackers play two touch.
b)   Support players throw the ball for the attackers to:
   - Head.
   - Volley.
   - Chest and volley.
   - Thigh and volley.

SUMMARY

1. The aim of this type of training is to improve a player's ability to perform highly intensive exercise for longer periods of time during a game and recover more quickly after high intensity exercise.

2. In this system, glycogen (carbohydrate) is released from the muscles into the blood stream in the form of glucose. This is a quick way of supplying energy in the absence of oxygen, but the disadvantage is that lactic acid is produced which accumulates in the blood, inhibits metabolism and causes rapid fatigue during high rates of activity.

3. Conditioning the lactic acid system enables the body to cope more easily with the accumulation of waste products and the negative aspects of this system.

4. The duration of the exercise period should not be less than 20 seconds and not more than 45 seconds so that extreme acidification does not occur. Since the lactic acid system is rarely active for more than 30 seconds at a time in a game of soccer, it seems pointless to make players carry out speed endurance work which takes them to the very limit.

5. The exercise intensity should be almost maximal and performed on an interval principle.

6. Players from lower leagues produce considerably less lactate than top class players, although even elite players do not experience much acidification during a game.

7. This type of training should have a low priority with amateur players since it is both physically and mentally demanding and, when time for training is limited, it can be put to better use.

8. Players under 16 should not use this type of training at all. Instead the coach should concentrate on technical training.

AEROBIC TRAINING

For fitness training, the coach must understand and identify the fitness requirements of the game. Jens Bangsbo, who used a video camera to film each player during an entire match, has analyzed the movements. According to his research, the average distance covered by outfield players is 10.8 kilometers, with a range from 9 to 14 kilometers. Much of this distance is covered by walking, jogging and low speed running, with only a small amount of time spent on moderate and high speed running and sprinting. However, this does not reflect the overall intensity of a game because players are also running backwards, changing direction, accelerating, decelerating, jumping and getting up from the ground.

A major part of the fitness program throughout the season has to be endurance training, but this must be related to the game. Steady state running for 20 minutes or more should be used during the off-season, in order to maintain basic fitness, but once the pre-season gets under way, aerobic training must be of a much higher intensity. The best way to do this is to use fixed intervals, with exercise periods of 1 to 5 minutes, followed by active rests of 1 to 3 minutes. The exercise period should also include stopping, starting, jumping, sitting down, running backwards, running sideways and accelerating and decelerating.

Unfortunately, many clubs think that a long run through the woods is still the best way to condition players. Although this will improve their aerobic endurance, research suggests that long runs at the same pace have a harmful effect on the muscles and nervous system. This type of work will recruit the intermediate fibers to assume the properties of slow twitch fibers and this will adversely affect peak power production. At the same time the nervous system becomes slower and less efficient in dealing with explosive soccer actions. Conversely, if intermittent high intensity aerobic work is used then this can train the intermediate fibers to take on the properties of fast twitch fibers. If runs are to be used, they should be no longer than 2 miles, not run on consecutive days and the pace varied throughout.

The best way to capitalize on the intermittent approach to training is by playing small-sided games. The intensity can be increased by changing the number of players, alternating the size of the field or changing the rules. Two touch, for example, will immediately increase the intensity of the game. It must be explained to the players that the priority of these games is to improve aerobic fitness. The shorter the exercise periods in these games, the higher the intensity must be, so it is vital that players only take rests during the natural breaks in the game.

Apart from aerobic fitness, the advantage of small-sided games it that they can help improve technique and tactical awareness, if the games themselves encourage vision and rapid decision making. However, for many coaches in the lower leagues it is not always possible to play small sided games for all sorts of reasons. For them there are many new high intensity aerobic activities included which do not require a ball and can be used in limited light and space.

INTERMITTENT AEROBIC TRAINING

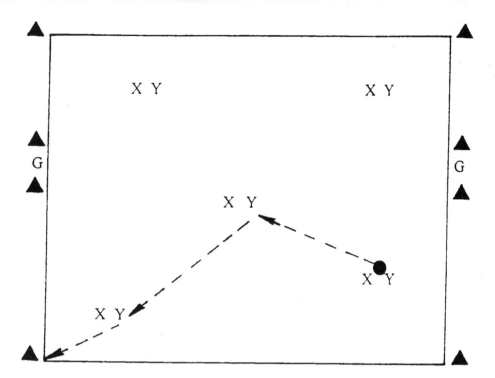

1. An area is marked out, with a cone in each corner acting as a goal and 2 normal goals, 8 yards wide at either end.
2. 4 to 8 outfield players and 2 goalkeepers take part and the size of the field is adjusted accordingly.
3. Each team has 2 cones and a goal to defend and 2 cones and a goal to attack.
4. If a team scores by striking a corner cone, they are awarded 1 point, but if they score in the normal goal, they get 3 points.
5. Normal soccer rules apply apart from this.

INTERMITTENT AEROBIC TRAINING

PRACTICE 2

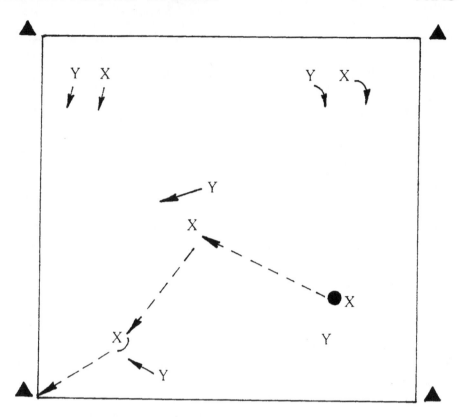

1. An area is marked out, with a cone in each corner acting as a goal.
2. Each team has 2 cones to defend and 2 cones to attack.
3. There are no goalkeepers and players are not allowed to handle the ball.
4. If a team scores by striking a cone with the ball, the players keep possession but must turn and attack the cones they have just been defending.

Variation

One team is given an extra player. If this team loses possession, the floating player immediately joins the opposing team.

INTERMITTENT AEROBIC TRAINING

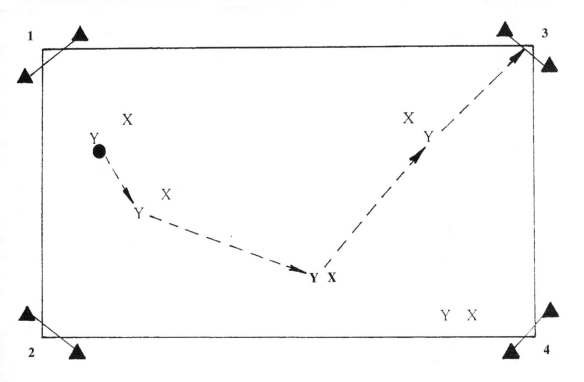

1. An area is marked out, with a goal at each corner, consisting of 2 cones about 1 yard wide.
2. Each team has 2 goals to defend and 2 goals to attack.
3. There are no goalkeepers and players are not allowed to handle the ball. Otherwise normal soccer rules apply.

Variations
a) 2 touch soccer only.
b) Man to man marking.
c) Teams attack 2 diagonal goals and defend 2 diagonal goals, e.g. X's try to score in goals 1 and 4 and defend goals 2 and 3.

INTERMITTENT AEROBIC TRAINING   PRACTICE 4

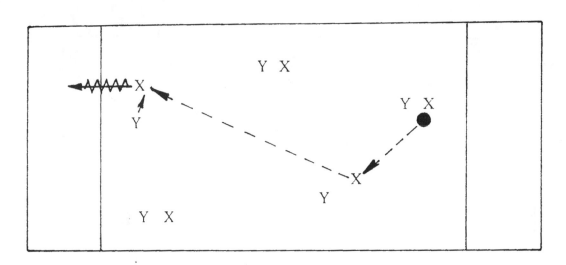

1. A game with zones for goals and 2 teams of 4 – 8 players.
2. The players of the team in possession of the ball pass it amongst themselves until they can set up a player to dribble the ball into the opposing zone and score by putting his foot on the ball.
3. The winner is the team with the most goals after a certain length of time.

Variation
Man to man marking.

INTERMITTENT AEROBIC TRAINING

PRACTICE 5

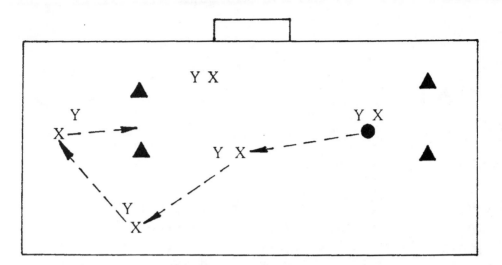

1. 2 teams of 4 – 8 players work on quarter of a field, with 2 goals, 40 yards apart, facing outwards to the sidelines.
2. There are no goalkeepers and handling is forbidden. Apart from that, normal rules apply.
3. A goal can only be scored from the reverse side of the goal.

Variations
a) 2 touch soccer between the goals, but normal soccer between the goals and the touch-line.
b) Normal soccer between the goals, but 2 touch between the touch-line and the goals.
c) Man to man marking.

INTERMITTENT AEROBIC TRAINING

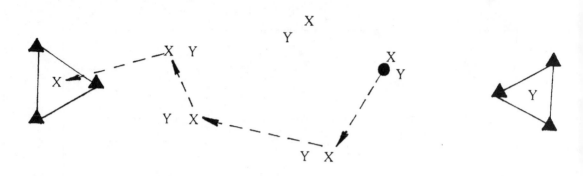

1. A game with 2 triangular goals made with cones and 2 teams of 5 – 8 players.
2. 1 player from each team stands in the triangle towards which his team is kicking.
3. The players of the team in possession of the ball pass it amongst themselves until they are able to chip the ball to their partner in the triangle.
4. He must catch it, without a bounce, for a goal to be scored.
5. The 'goalkeeper' restarts the game by throwing the ball out to a member of the opposing team.
6. The goalkeeper should be replaced at regular intervals.

INTERMITTENT AEROBIC TRAINING   PRACTICE 7

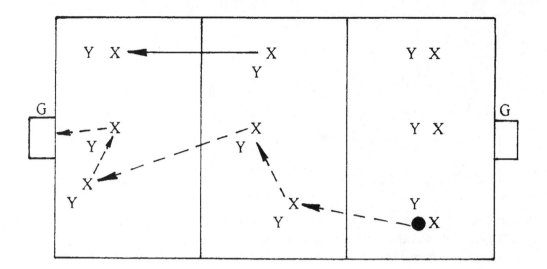

1. Half a field is divided into 3 equal zones, with 2 full sized goals placed on the side lines.
2. Both teams are divided into groups of 3, with each group lining up in a zone.
3. In the end goal-zones, 3 attackers against 3 defenders, while in the center zone, 3 mid-field players oppose each other.
4. The ball is passed from zone to zone, with the aim of scoring goals at one end and not conceding any at the other.

Variations
a) Once the ball is in the end zone, a mid-field player can join the attacking team.
b) The number in each zone can vary in order to replicate the playing strategy of the team e.g. 4-4-2, 4-3-3 etc.

INTERMITTENT AEROBIC TRAINING PRACTICE 8

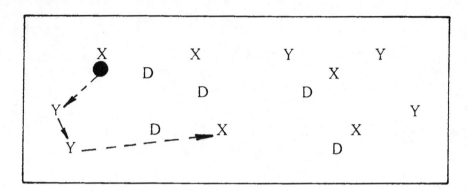

1. 2 teams of 4,5 or 6 players play against 1 team of 4,5 or 6 players, on quarter of a soccer field. All 3 teams must be distinctively marked.
2. The defending team tries to touch the ball. If they succeed, the players who lost the ball become the defending team.
3. No goals or points are awarded in this game. The defending team, however, must be encouraged to work hard to regain possession.

Variations
a) 2 touch only for the attacking teams.
b) The ball must be passed alternately between the attacking teams.

INTERMITTENT AEROBIC TRAINING   PRACTICE 9

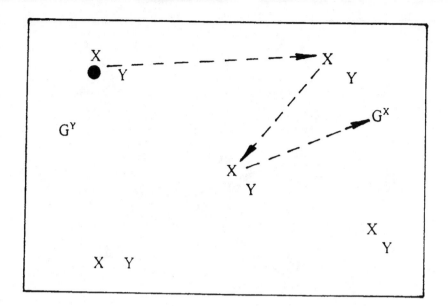

1. 2 teams of 4 to 8 players, plus 2 goalkeepers, work on a quarter of a soccer field.
2. A goalkeeper is assigned to each team and is allowed to move freely around the area.
3. Each team tries to keep possession and score a point by passing to their goalkeeper.
4. It helps if a point is scored for 8 consecutive passes, as this keeps defenders from man marking the goalkeepers.

INTERMITTENT AEROBIC TRAINING

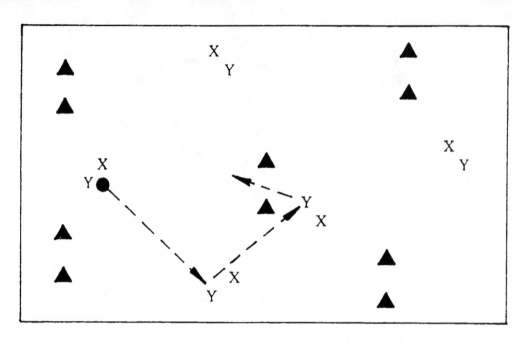

1. 2 teams of 3 – 5 players work on a quarter of a soccer field.
2. Several small goals, 1 yard wide and made with cones, are placed around the field.
3. Both teams attempt to keep possession and shoot through one of the goals to score.
4. A team cannot score consecutively in the same goal.

Variations
a) A shot through the goal must reach a member of the same team.
b) A goal is awarded if a wall pass is played by the goal scorer and receiver.

INTERMITTENT AEROBIC TRAINING   **PRACTICE 11**

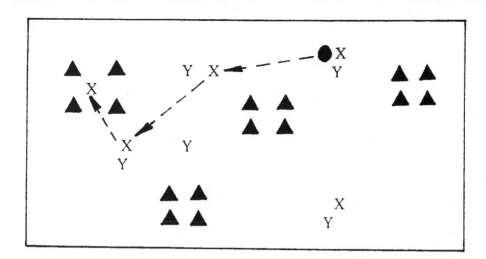

1. 2 teams of 3 – 5 players work on a quarter of a soccer field.
2. Several 2 yard squares, made with cones, are placed around the field.
3. A team scores a point if one of it's players enters a square and receives a pass from a teammate.
4. A team cannot score consecutively in the same square.

Variation

A point is scored if the player in the square receives the ball and passes first time to a teammate. An extra point is awarded for a wall pass.

INTERMITTENT AEROBIC TRAINING

PRACTICE 12

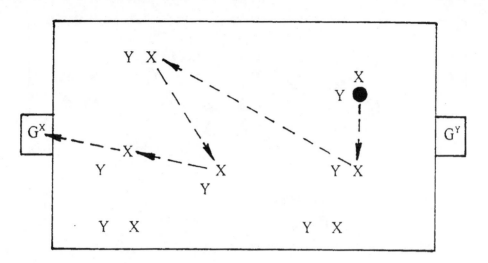

1. 2 teams of 6 – 10 players work on half a field, with 2 full size goals placed on the touch lines, and 2 goalkeepers.
2. The aim of both teams is to pass the ball to their goalkeeper, who is placed in the goal they are attacking.
3. To score a point, the goalkeeper must collect the ball within the line of the posts. If he collects outside the line, no points are awarded.
4. After collecting the ball, the goalkeeper immediately throws it to the opposition.

Variation

This game can also be used as a closing down practice. The nearest defender to the ball is encouraged to close the attacker down and try to prevent the ball from going forward.

INTERMITTENT AEROBIC TRAINING

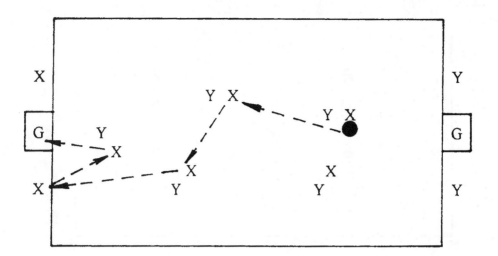

1. 2 teams of 4 – 8 players work on quarter of a field, with 2 full size goals and 2 goal-keepers.
2. A target man is placed on either side of each goal.
3. The attacking team can play off the target men, who have 1 touch to return the ball into the goal mouth for a possible shot at goal.
4. Change the target men frequently.

INTERMITTENT AEROBIC TRAINING

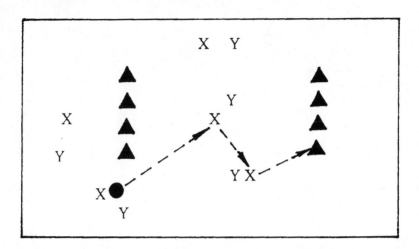

1. 2 teams of 4 – 8 players work on quarter of a soccer field.
2. Each team defends a row of cones and attacks the other.
3. There should be a minimum of 4 cones, positioned in a line, about 1 yard apart. The aim is to knock over a cone of the opposing team with the ball.
4. Every time they succeed, they score a point.
5. Play is allowed in front of and behind the cones.

Variations
a) Man to man marking.
b) 2 touch between the cones, normal soccer behind the cones.
c) Normal soccer between the cones, 2 touch behind the cones.

INTERMITTENT AEROBIC TRAINING   **PRACTICE 15**

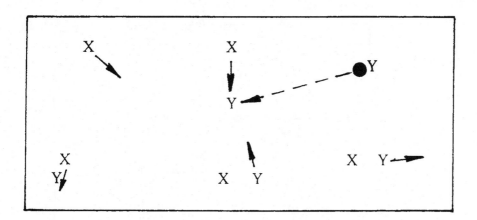

1. 2 equal teams without goals.
2. The Y's start with the ball and attempt to keep possession.
3. If they succeed in making 6 consecutive passes they earn a point.
4. If the X's gain possession either by interception, a tackle, or the ball going out of play, then they attempt to get 6 consecutive passes and earn a point.

Variations
a) Man to man marking.
b) A successful wall pass is awarded an extra pass.
c) The above practice can be used, but with the players in both teams numbered 1 to 6. The team then has to pass in sequence to gain a point.

INTERMITTENT AEROBIC TRAINING

PRACTICE 16

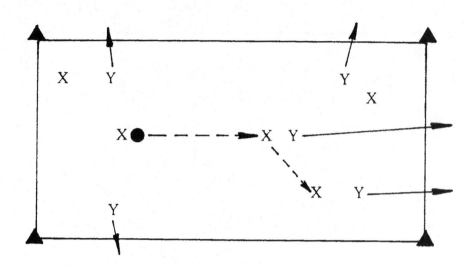

1. 2 equal teams without goals. The playing area is marked out with 4 cones.
2. One team starts with the ball and attempts to keep possession.
3. On a signal from the coach, the team without the ball must run around the marked area before attempting to regain possession.
4. They have 1 minute to do this, but if not successful they must repeat the exercise.
5. The 'penalty run' should motivate players to work hard to gain possession.

INTERMITTENT AEROBIC TRAINING   PRACTICE 17

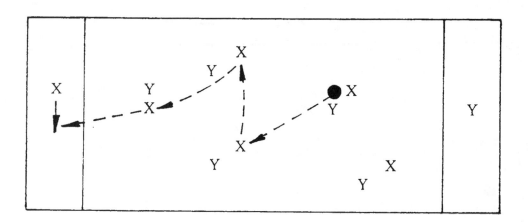

1. 2 teams of 5 – 10 players work on half a soccer field, which has 2 outer zones about 5 yards wide on each touch line.
2. A player from each team is placed in one of the outer zones and is free to move any-where in it. The players from his team attempt to pass the ball to him.
3. A point is scored for every successful pass to the player in the outer zone.
4. When a point is scored, the outer player transfers the ball to the opposing team.
5. The outfield players are not allowed to enter the end zones.
6. Change the outer players regularly.

Variations
a) Man to man marking.
b) The number of ball touches per player is limited e.g. 3 touches only.
c) All players from the attacking team must be in the opponent's half of the field when the ball is passed to the player in the outer zone for a point to be scored.

INTERMITTENT AEROBIC TRAINING

PRACTICE 18

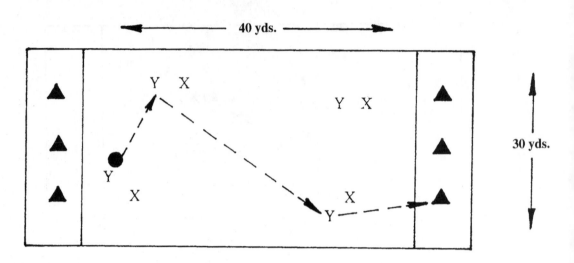

1. 2 teams of 3 – 5 players work in an area approximately 40 yards by 30 yards. A zone 2 yards wide is placed at both ends of the field and 3 cones, equal distance apart, are placed in each zone.
2. Both teams defend their own cones and try to hit their opponent's cones with the ball. A goal is scored for every cone hit.
3. The zone area may not be entered by defenders or attackers.

Variations
a) Man to man marking.
b) The number of ball touches per player is limited e.g. 2 touches only.
c) The distance between the cones can vary.

INTERMITTENT AEROBIC TRAINING PRACTICE 19

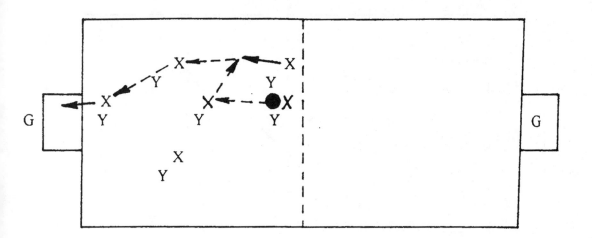

1. 2 teams of 6 – 10 players work on half a field, with 2 full size goals placed on the touch lines. A half-way line is marked out.
2. To score a goal, all the attacking players must be in their opponent's half of the field. If a goal is scored, but an attacking player is still in his own half, then the goal does not count.
3. If a goal is scored and a defending player is not in his own half, then the goal counts as 2.

Variations
a) Man to man marking.
b) The number of ball touches per player is limited e.g. 1 touch.

INTERMITTENT AEROBIC TRAINING   PRACTICE 20

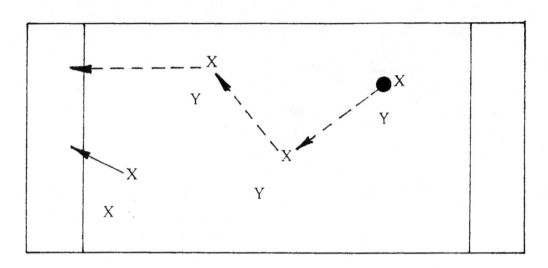

1. 2 teams of 3 – 5 work on a quarter of a soccer field, which has two 10 yd zones marked at either end.
2. The attacking team attempts to pass the ball into the opponent's zone and get one of its players to bring the ball under control before it goes out of play. A point is awarded if this occurs.
3. The defending team is not allowed into its own zone.

Variations
a) Man to man marking.
b) The number of ball touches per player is limited e.g. 2 touches.

INTERMITTENT AEROBIC TRAINING   **PRACTICE 21**

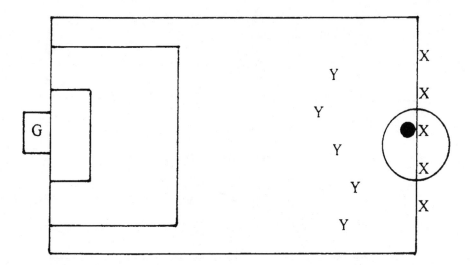

1. 2 teams of 4 – 6 players, plus a goalkeeper, work on half a field.
2. Normal soccer rules apply, including off-sides.
3. X's start with the ball on the half-way line and use various tactical methods to try to score.
4. If X's lose possession, they become the defending team.
5. However, the ball is not in play again until all the Y's are back on the half-way line. It is vital that they regroup quickly, so that the intensity of the game is maintained.
6. If X's score, then they maintain possession and start again on the half-way line.

Variation
One team attacks for a set time e.g. 5 minutes, then becomes the defending team.

INTERMITTENT AEROBIC TRAINING   PRACTICE 22

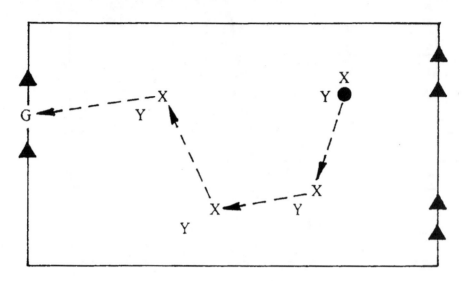

1. 9 or more players work on a field, 40 yards by 30 yards. There is a full size goal with a goalkeeper at one end and 2 small goals, 2 yards wide and 20 yards apart, at the other.
2. The number of outfield players in each team must be the same.
3. X's start by attacking the full size goal and defending the 2 small goals.
4. After a set time, the players change ends, apart from the goalkeeper. X's now defend the large goal and attack the 2 small goals.

Variations
a) Man to man marking.
b) A limited number of touches on the ball e.g. 3 touches.
c) No passing above head height.

INTERMITTENT AEROBIC TRAINING

PRACTICE 23

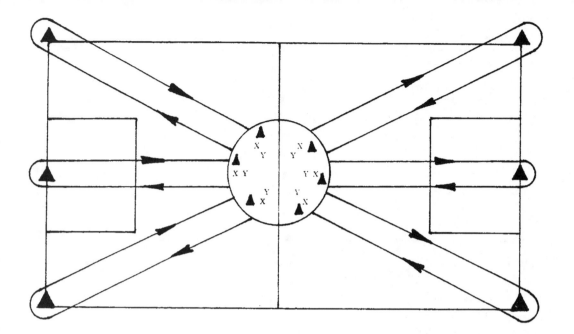

1. 6 cones are placed on 4 corners of the field and in each goal mouth.
2. The X's start in the center circle and, on a signal from the coach, run around the cone they are facing and back to the middle.
3. The players then run clockwise to the next cone and continue until all 6 cones have been visited.
4. On returning from each cone, one foot must be placed in the center circle.
5. When X's finish their run, Y's start and complete the same course.
6. Players work for a set time or set number of circuits, depending on the fitness levels of the group.

Variations

a) Players run in a counter-clockwise direction.
b) After X's have run to a cone and back, they hand over to Y's who run the same course. This pattern is repeated until all 6 cones have been visited.

INTERMITTENT AEROBIC TRAINING

PRACTICE 24

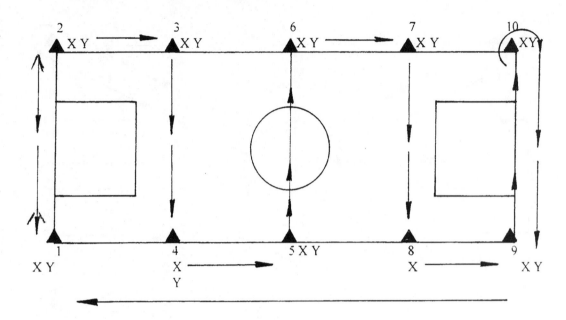

1. Any number of pairs stand by a cone, as positioned on the diagram.
2. On a signal from the coach, X's start and run the course indicated, as fast as possible.
3. The aim is to get back before the other runners.
4. When X's finish, Y's start and complete the same course.
5. The exercise periods (one around) last for about 2 minutes, with 2 minutes rest. Total duration could be 24 minutes (6 rounds) depending on the fitness levels of the group.

INTERMITTENT AEROBIC TRAINING PRACTICE 25

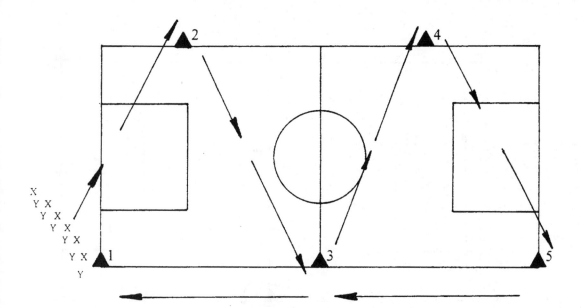

1. 5 cones are positioned as in the diagram.
2. All the X's line up on cone 1 and on a signal from the coach, run the course
   indicated, until they are back at the start.
3. When all the X's have finished, Y's start and complete the same course.
4. Players work for a set time (20 minutes) or set number of circuits (8). Depending on
   the fitness levels of the group.

INTERMITTENT AEROBIC TRAINING **PRACTICE 26**

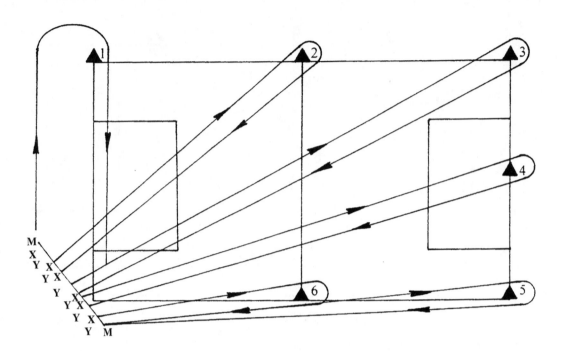

1. 6 cones are placed on 3 corners of the field, on the half-way line and in the goal mouth.
2. X's start in one corner of the field and on a signal from the coach, run around the cone they are facing and back to base.
3. The players then run clockwise to the next cone and continue until all 6 cones have been visited.
4. On returning from each cone, one foot must cross the base line.
5. When X's finish their run. Y's start and complete the same course.
6. Players work for a set time (25 minutes) or set number of circuits (5), depending on their level of fitness.

Variations
a) Players run in a counter-clockwise direction.
b) After X's have run to a cone and back, they hand over to Y's, who run the same course. This pattern continues until all 6 cones have been visited.

INTERMITTENT AEROBIC TRAINING   **PRACTICE 27**

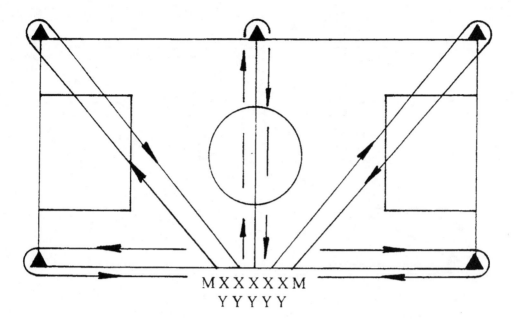

1. 5 cones are placed on 4 corners of the field and the half-way line.
2. X's start between 2 markers on the half-way line and on a signal from the coach, run around the cone they are facing and back to base.
3. The players then run clockwise to the next cone and continue until all 5 cones have been visited.
4. On returning from each cone, one foot must cross the base line.
5. When X's finish their run, Y's start and complete the same course.
6. Players work for a set time or set number of circuits, depending on their level of fitness.

Variations
a) Players run in a counter-clockwise direction.
b) After X's have run to a cone and back, the Y's run the same course. This pattern continues until they have visited each cone.
c) Players may visit the cones in any order they wish.

INTERMITTENT AEROBIC TRAINING

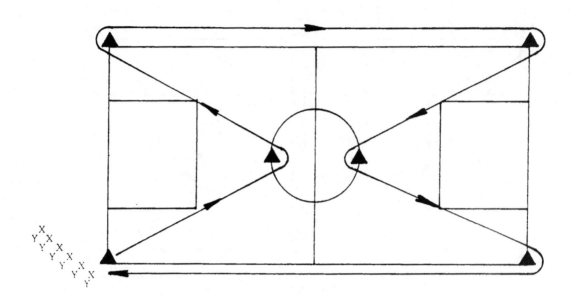

1. 6 cones are placed on 4 corners of the field and in the center circle.
2. X's start in one corner of the field and on a signal from the coach, run 1 lap of the course indicated, as fast as possible.
3. When X's finish, Y's start and complete the same course.
4. Players work for a set number of circuits (e.g. 6), depending on their level of fitness.

Variations
a) Players work in a counter-clockwise direction.
b) Players complete 2 circuits.
c) During the run, players sit down, touch the ground with both hands, sprint, jump in the air, etc. This makes the exercise far more demanding.

INTERMITTENT AEROBIC TRAINING   **PRACTICE 29**

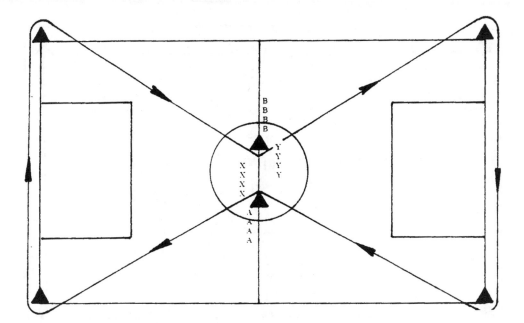

1. 6 cones are placed on the 4 corners of the field and on the half-way line as shown.
2. X's and Y's start at the same time and run 1 lap in opposite directions, following the course shown in the diagram. The aim is to beat the other group back.
3. When X's and Y's have completed 1 lap, A's and B's start, with A's following the same course as the X's and B's the same course as the Y's.
4. Players work for a set time or a set number of laps.

Variations
a) Players run in a counter-clockwise direction.
b) Each group covers 1/2 lap on the first run, then 1, 1 1/2, 2, 2 1/2, and 3 laps.

INTERMITTENT AEROBIC TRAINING

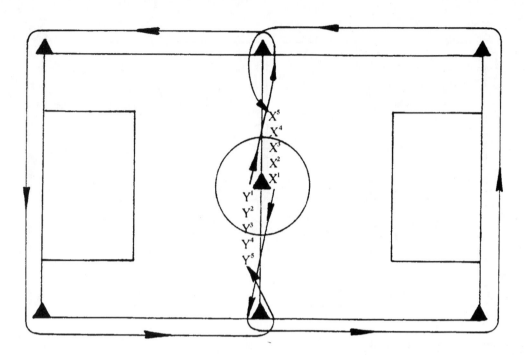

1. 7 cones are placed around the field, with 4 on the corners and 3 on the half-way line.
2. X1 and Y1 each place a hand on the central cone and, on a signal from the coach, set off at the same time, run half a lap of the field in the direction indicated and attempt to beat each other back.
3. As soon as X1 and Y1 have started, X2 and Y2 move forward, touch the cone and begin 3 seconds after X1 and Y1.
4. Each pair follows the same pattern until everybody has completed the run.
5. The work and rest periods are equal.
6. Players work for a set number of laps.

Variations
a) Players work in the opposite direction after each run.
b) The players cover 1/2 a lap on the first run, then 1, 1 1/2, 2, 1 1/2 , 1 and 1/2 a lap.

INTERMITTENT AEROBIC TRAINING   **PRACTICE 31**

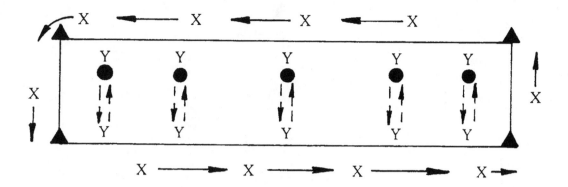

1. An area of 40 yards by 10 yards is marked out with 4 cones.
2. The players are divided into pairs and on a signal from the coach, the X's run in a counter-clockwise direction around the running area.
3. Meanwhile the Y's have the ball between 2 cones and perform an active recovery by passing to each other.
4. When X's have completed 3 laps, Y's start and run the same course.
5. The X's then perform an active recovery by passing in pairs.
6. Players work for a set time or set number of laps.

Variations
a) Players work in a clockwise direction.
b) Each player covers 5 laps on the first run, then 4, 3, 2, 1, 2, 3, 4, 5.

INTERMITTENT AEROBIC TRAINING   **PRACTICE 32**

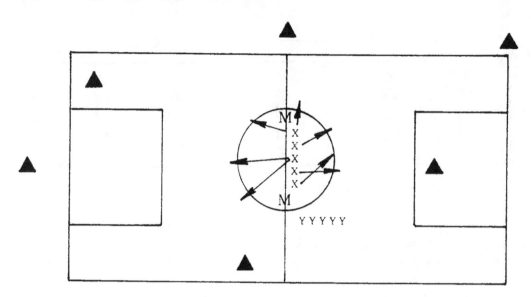

1. 6 cones are positioned at random on and off the field. 2 markers are placed on the halfway line to act as a base.
2. X's line up at the base and on a signal from the coach, set off to run around all 6 cones.
3. However, each time they visit a cone, they must return to base before setting off for the next one.
4. Players may visit the cones in any order they wish.
5. When all the X's have finished, the Y's start and complete the same run in any order.
6. Work for a set number of runs.

INTERMITTENT AEROBIC TRAINING

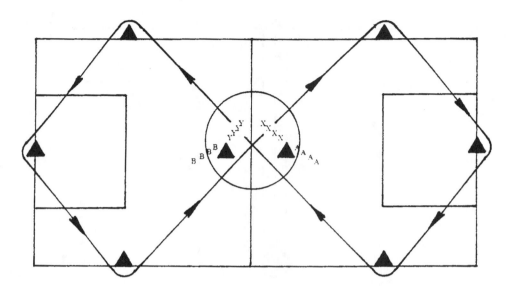

1. 8 cones are placed around the field, with 4 on the touch line, 2 in the goal mouths and 2 in the center circle.
2. X's and Y's line up on their respective cones. On a signal from the coach they set off and run the course indicated in the diagram. X's work in a clockwise direction at the start and Y's in a counter-clockwise direction.
3. When X's and Y's have completed 1 lap, A's and B's start, with A's following the same course as X's and B's the same course as Y's.
4. It is important that players are aware of each other as they pass between the markers after 1/2 lap.
5. Players work for a set number of laps.

Variations
a) Players complete 2 laps then hand over the exercise to the other team.
b) Players work for a set time e.g. 90 seconds.

INTERMITTENT AEROBIC TRAINING

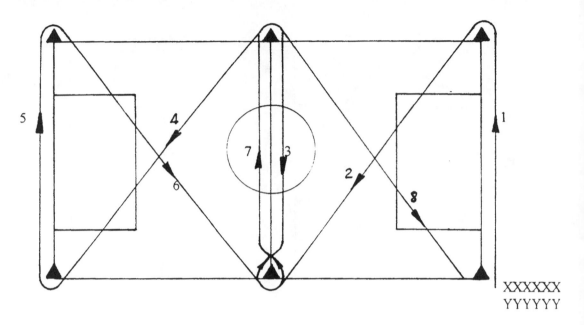

1. 6 cones are placed on the 4 corners of the field and on the halfway line, as shown in the diagram.
2. X's line up at the start and, on a signal from the coach, run the course indicated.
3. When all the X's have completed the run, the Y's start and follow the same course.
4. Players work for a set number of laps.

INTERMITTENT AEROBIC TRAINING

PRACTICE 35

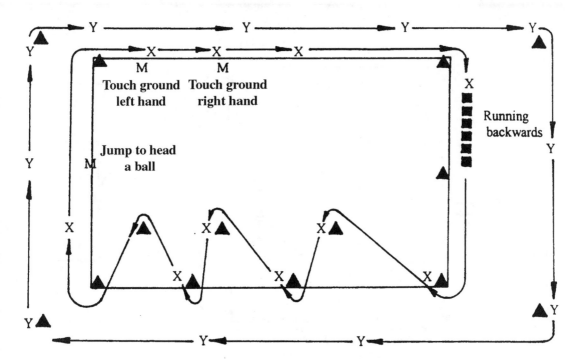

1. A course 40 yards by 30 yards marked out with 13 cones, positioned as shown. 4 more cones are placed 8 yards from the corners of the running area and these mark the edge of the recovery zone.
2. X's line up in the running area and on a signal from the coach, run in the direction shown. The Y's jog around the recovery zone.
3. At certain markers on the course, players perform set exercises.
4. X's work for 1 minute, then change places with Y's and jog around the recovery zone.
5. Players work for a set time (e.g. 24 – 30 minutes).

INTERMITTENT AEROBIC TRAINING

PRACTICE 36

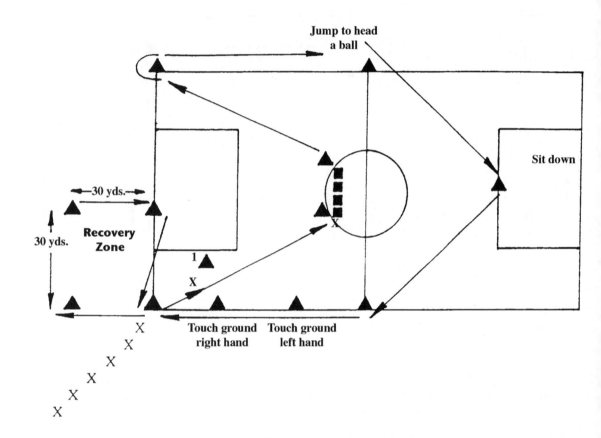

1. A course is marked out with 10 cones as shown in the diagram. 3 more cones, plus the start and finish cone, mark the edge of the recovery zone.
2. Players line up in single file at the starting cone. On a signal from the coach, the first player runs the course in the direction shown.
3. When he reaches cone 1, the next player starts.
4. At certain cones around the course, players perform set exercises.
5. When runners have completed the course, they are given 60 seconds to walk around the recovery zone.
6. Players work for a set number of runs (e.g. 6), depending on their level of fitness.

INTERMITTENT AEROBIC TRAINING

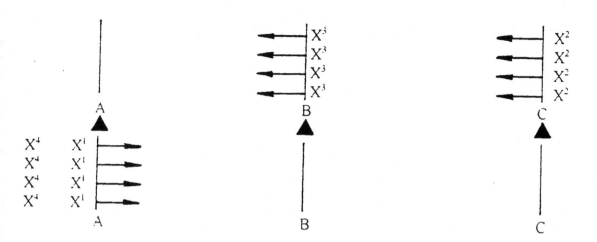

1. 3 lines are marked as in the diagram. The outer lines (A and C) are 60 yards apart.
2. X1's start on a signal from the coach and run to line C. The running speed should be high, but one the players can maintain for several exercise periods.
3. When the last runner has passed line C, X2's start and run to line B.
4. When the last runner has passed line B, X3's start and run to line A.
5. When the last runner has passed line A, X4's start and run to line C.
6. The exercise continues for 3 sets of 6 minutes with 1 minute rest between sets.

Variations

On the run from line A to line C, the players can perform the following exercises at line B.

a) Jump in the air.
b) Touch the ground with both hands.
c) Stop, then run again.
d) Sit down.
e) Do a complete turn.
f) Cut right 3 paces.
g) Cut left 3 paces.
h) Slide laterally to the right 2 paces.
i) Slide laterally to the left 2 paces.

INTERMITTENT AEROBIC TRAINING

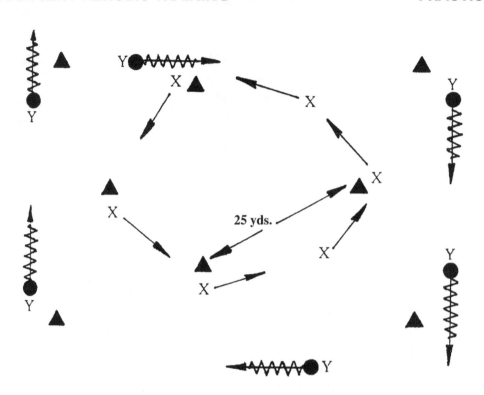

1. A course is marked out in a diamond shape, with 4 cones, which are 25 yards apart. 4 more cones are placed outside the running area and these mark the edge of the recovery zone.
2. X's line up in the running area and on a signal from the coach, run in the direction shown.
3. During the run, the coach shouts out a series of exercises, which must be performed. The exercises should relate to the game e.g. jump in the air to head a ball, touch the ground with both hands, sit down, run in the opposite direction, stop and start, walk, sprint, run sideways, speed up, slow down, etc.
4. Y's, meantime, jog in a clockwise direction, dribbling a ball.
5. X's work for 1 minute then change places with the Y's and jog around the recovery zone, dribbling a ball.
6. The working players always start by running in a counter-clockwise direction, while the recovering players always dribble in a clockwise direction.
7. Players work for a set time(e.g. 20 – 30 minutes) depending on the fitness levels of the group.

INTERMITTENT AEROBIC TRAINING

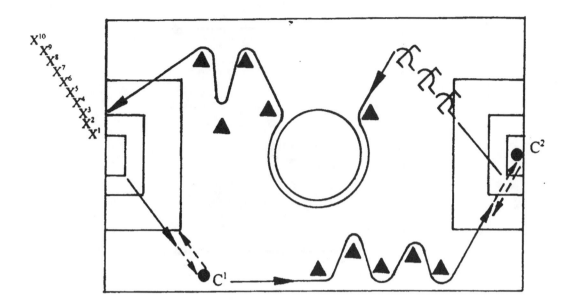

1. A course is marked out with 10 cones and 3 hurdles. Two coaches, with a ball each, are positioned as shown.
2. X's line up in single file at the goal. On a signal, the first player sprints to the coach, plays a 1 / 2, then runs the course in the direction shown.
3. As soon as X1 has passed back to C1, the next player starts.
4. When runners have completed the course, which includes running through the cones, playing a 1 / 2 with C2, jumping the hurdles, running around the center circle, running around more cones and sprinting back to the start, they rejoin the back of the line.
5. Players work for a set number of runs (e.g. 6), depending on their level of fitness.

Variations
a) The coaches throw the ball for the players to volley.
b) The coaches throw the ball for the players to head.

INTERMITTENT AEROBIC TRAINING   **PRACTICE 40**

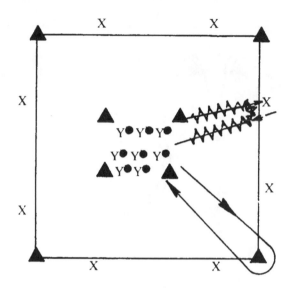

1. An area 30 yards by 30 yards is marked out with 4 cones. Inside this area, a 10 yard by 10 yard square is marked out.
2. The Y's have a ball each and start in the small square.
3. They dribble at speed to any of the X's on the outside of the large square, play a 1 / 2, then dribble back to the center where they leave their balls.
4. They then run around any one of the corner cones in the large square and back to the center, where they collect their balls again.
5. They then dribble to another X and repeat the passing drill, but it cannot be to the same side that they dribbled the last time.
6. Y's follow this sequence of working with the ball and without the ball for 3 minutes before changing with the X's on the outside.
7. Players work for a set number of runs (e.g. 4) depending on their level of fitness.

INTERMITTENT AEROBIC TRAINING   **PRACTICE 41**

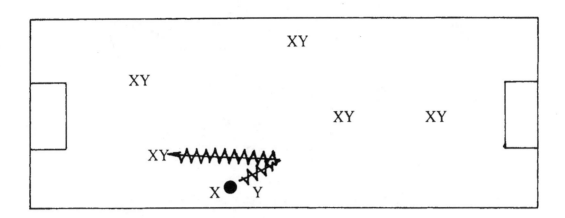

1. 12 to 22 players play a normal game of soccer on half a field. A goal is placed on each touch line.
2. During the game the coach will blow a whistle and the teams will immediately reverse roles and play in the opposite direction.
3. The goalkeepers do not change ends but defend against whichever team is attacking their goal.
4. As soon as the whistle blows, those defending must contain the attack until other defenders can get back.
5. This game is physically demanding so the coach should be realistic in the number of times he blows the whistle.

INTERMITTENT AEROBIC TRAINING

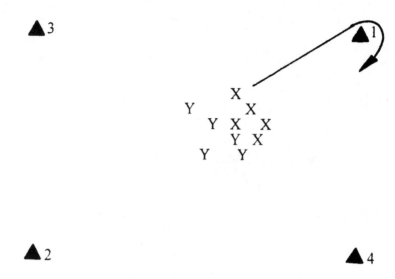

1. A square 30 yards by 30 yards is marked out by 4 cones. All players start in the middle of the square.
2. On a signal from the coach, the X's run around each cone in the order indicated. They always run to the left of the cone in order to avoid collisions.
3. When all the X's arrive back, the Y's complete the same course.
4. When all the Y's have returned, the X's then dribble the course, making sure their balls do not touch those of other players.
5. Y's then repeat X's actions by dribbling the course.
6. Players repeat this sequence of running and dribbling for a set time or set number of laps.

Variation

X's and Y's start at the same time and run or dribble the course in opposite directions. Thus one team will run around the cones in the following order: 1, 2, 3, 4, while the other team uses the opposite order: 4, 3, 2, 1.

INTERMITTENT AEROBIC TRAINING   PRACTICE 43

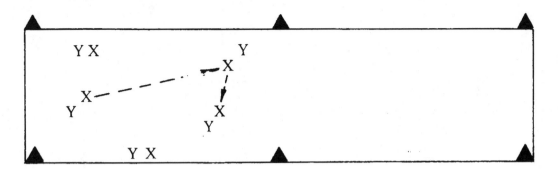

1. The game is played in an area 50 yards by 30 yards, which is divided in half, forming an adjacent 30 yds by 25 yds grid. 6 cones mark the corners and mid-field.
2. One team is positioned within its own possession area and tries to keep the ball.
3. The opponents try to gain possession and, if successful, they dribble or pass to their own area. Here they try to maintain possession of the ball.
4. Each time a team completes 10 consecutive passes in its own area, it scores one point.
5. Work for 6 minutes and rest for two minutes. This sequence should be repeated 3 times.

INTERMITTENT AEROBIC TRAINING

PRACTICE 44

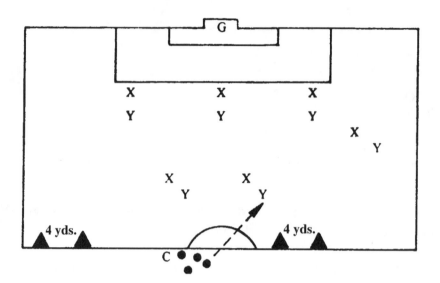

1. The game is played on half a field, with one normal goal and a goalkeeper and two smaller goals, about 4 yards wide, on the halfway line.
2. A minimum of 12 players plus a goalkeeper is required for this game.
3. The coach positions himself on the halfway line, with a number of balls.
4. Y's attack the goal first and if they score they maintain possession, with the coach feeding the next ball in to them.
5. If X's intercept, they attempt to dribble through either of the smaller goals. If successful, they become the attackers.
6. Only goals scored in the normal goal count.

Variations

a)   If the defenders gain possession and pass the ball to a teammate through either of the smaller goals, then they get a chance to attack the normal goal.

b)   One team attacks the normal goal for a set length of time. Goals scored in the two smaller goals also count.

INTERMITTENT AEROBIC TRAINING

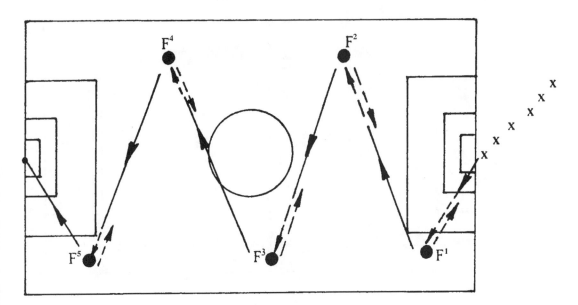

1. 5 feeders position themselves, as in the diagram, with a ball each. The working players line up in single file at the goal.
2. On a signal the first player sprints to F1, plays a 1 / 2, then does the same with the other feeders, in the order shown. After playing a 1 / 2 with F5, he runs to the goal and waits for the other players to complete the course.
3. As soon as the first player has played a 1 / 2 with F1, the next player starts.
4. When all the players have reached the opposite goal, the first player repeats the course in the opposite direction.
5. Players work for a set number of runs (e.g. 4) or set time.

Variation
The feeders throw balls for headers or volleys.

INTERMITTENT AEROBIC TRAINING

PRACTICE 46

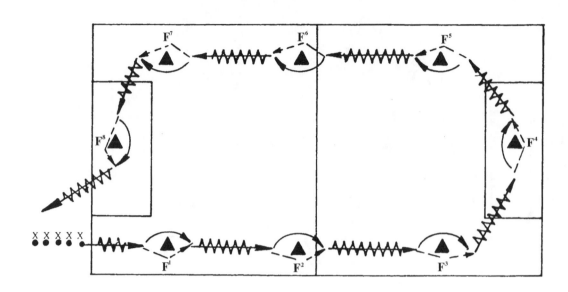

1. 8 feeders position themselves, as in the diagram, with a cone in front of each.
2. The working players line up on the goal line with a ball each.
3. On a signal from the coach, the first player dribbles to F1, plays a wall pass, collects his ball and then does the same with each feeder in the order shown.
4. As soon as the first player has wall passed with F1, the next player starts.
5. Players work for a set number of laps (e.g. 3) or set time, then change roles.

Variations
a) Players work the other way around e.g. F8 first.
b) Players pass the ball and jump the cone before collecting the return.
c) Two groups of players line up on opposite goal lines and start at the same time. Thus one group will work to F1 first, while the other group works to F5 first.

INTERMITTENT AEROBIC TRAINING

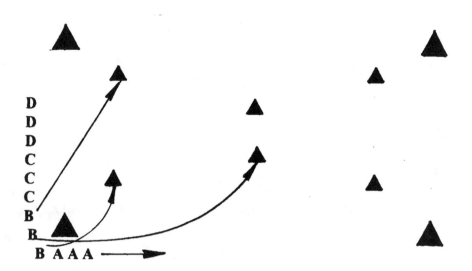

1. An area of 30 yards by 20 yards is marked out with 4 cones. 6 small cones are positioned at random within the rectangle.
2. The players are divided into groups of 3 or 4, and jog around the outside of the marked area.
3. On a signal from the coach, one of the groups (in this example, B) runs into the area and touches all 6 cones as quickly as possible.
4. When the players have visited every cone, they rejoin the back of the jogging group and the coach calls for another group to do the same.
5. Players work for a set time, according to the fitness level of the group.

Variations

The sprinting group must:
a)   Run around each cone.
b)   Jump over each cone.
c)   Jump over each cone and do a 180° turn.
d)   Jump forwards and backwards over each cone.
e)   Tackle each cone.
f)   Dribble the ball to each cone.
g)   Dribble around each cone.

INTERMITTENT AEROBIC TRAINING
PRACTICE 48

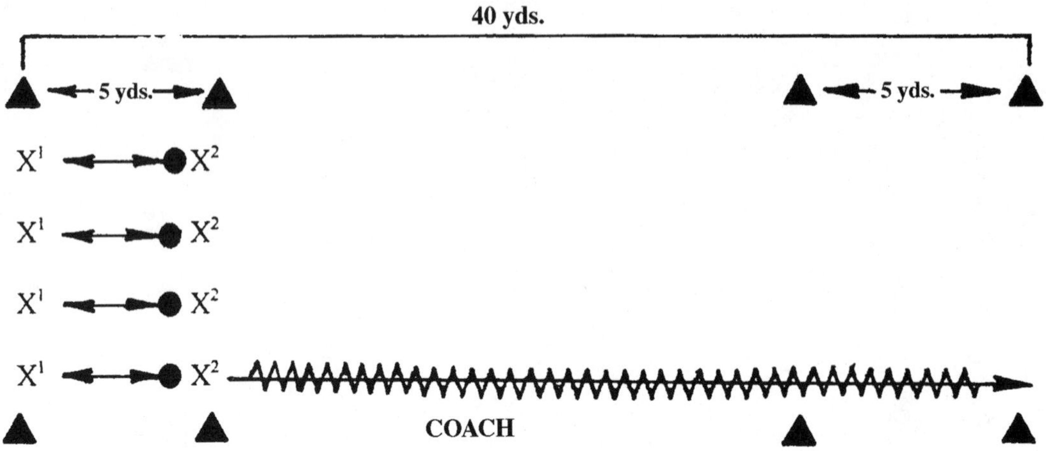

1. 8 cones are set up as shown in the diagram.
2. Players work in pairs, as in the diagram, and pass a ball to each other.
3. On a signal from the coach, X2's spin with the ball and dribble at speed to cone 4. X1's follow 5 yards behind.
4. The same passing sequence is repeated at cones 3 and 4 for a short time.
5. On a signal from the coach, X1 spins with the ball and dribbles at speed to cone 1, and the process starts again.
6. Players work for 3 minutes before getting 1 minute rest.

Variations
a) The dribbling player does a double check with the ball. The running player runs backwards 4 steps at the same time.
b) The running player sprints in an arc.

INTERMITTENT AEROBIC TRAINING   **PRACTICE 49**

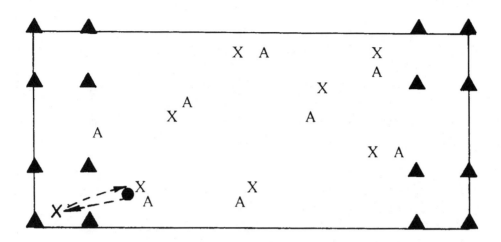

1. Two teams of 6 – 10 players work on half a field. Four 10 yard squares are set up in each corner of the field and these act as goals.
2. A goal is scored if the ball is passed into the square and then out to a teammate.
3. Both teams can score in any of the 4 goals.
4. Players cannot wait in the square.

Variations
a) Man to man marking.
b) A goal is scored if a player dribbles in and out of the square.
c) Passing goals have to be touched by 3 players.
d) Each team has two goals to defend and two to attack.

SUMMARY

1. The aims of this type of training are to improve the oxygen transport system, increase the ability of the muscles to use oxygen and help players recover quickly after high intensity exercise.
2. The best way to make the most of the intermittent approach to training is by playing small-sided games.
3. In these games, the intensity of the training can be changed by adjusting the rules, altering the size of the field, or increasing or decreasing the number of players. For example, one or two touch soccer or man to man marking will increase intensity, while 8 v 8 on half a field and no limitation on touches will decrease the intensity.
4. If intensity is required, then the coach should use fixed intervals between 3 and 5 minutes, followed by active recovery.
5. If a high endurance capacity is required, then continuous exercise is needed. The players should only take rests during natural breaks in the game.
6. For lower leagues, it is important that the overload principle is maintained. If the players do not have the soccer skills to cope with one or two touch passing or man to man marking, then the game will be continually interrupted and the aim of the session not achieved. The coach must therefore adapt the rules or increase the size of the field in order to give players more time and space.
7. Aerobic training sessions can also be carried out without a ball. However, these drills must be soccer related and must include running backwards, changing direction, accelerating, decelerating, jumping and getting up from the ground. It is vital that players do not get into steady state running.
8. Children between 8 and 14 must enjoy themselves and so the emphasis should be on playing soccer. The running activities in this section are therefore inappropriate for this age group.
9. The games, however, are appropriate but are best developed in small-sided matches such as 4 v 4. Although the size of the field should be adjusted to the children's ability, the players should not be restricted by one touch soccer or man to man marking.
10. The games should allow children to recognize situations and to come up with their own solutions to the problems. The coach is there to guide and encourage, not to dictate and over-coach!
11. From 14 to 18, as players go through their growth spurts, physical conditioning becomes more relevant, since aerobic fitness, strength and speed can now be developed. However, endurance is still best improved by playing small-sided games, with the rules adjusted to increase the intensity of the practice.

The training ideas portrayed in this book will be useful for any coach dealing with footballers from a junior and a professional level. The practices can only enhance fitness and improve individual and team performance.

Kit Symons
Fulham and Wales

Training in soccer is far more beneficial if the sessions are game related. This book offers coaches the opportunity to improve their players' fitness and make the training sessions more informative and enjoyable.

Steven Guppy
Leicester City and England 'B'

VIDEOS by Roger Wilkinson

#205 Soccer Success
One-on-One Coaching for Parent and Playe • $29.95
by Roger Wilkinson

#722   Soccer Success: Tape 2
Coaching the Advanced Player • $29.95
by Roger Wilkinson

#919   Soccer Success: Tape 3
Coaching the Youth Team • $29.95
by Roger Wilkinson

REEDSWAIN BOOKS

#789 The Soccer Scouting Guide • $12.95
by Joe Bertuzzi

#793 Coaching the 5-3-2 with a Sweeper • $14.95
by Fascetti and Scaia

#788 ZONE PLAY • $14.95
A Technical and Tactical Handbook

#225 The Sweeper • $9.95
by Richard Bate
$9.95

#256 The Creative Dribbler • $14.95
by Peter Schreiner

#169 Coaching Advanced Soccer Players • $12.95
by Richard Bate

#264 Coaching 6 to 10 Year Olds • $14.95
by Giuliano Rusca

#785 Complete Book of Soccer Restart Plays • $14.95
by Mario Bonfanti and Angelo Pereni

#792 120 Competitive Games and Exercises for Soccer
$14.95
by Nicola Pica

#905 Soccer Strategies: Defensive and Attacking Tactics
$12.95
by Robyn Jones

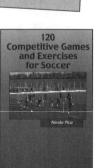

1.800.331.5191 or visit our
Web Site at www.reedswain.com